Praise for *Free Trade Rocks!*...

"Ever since Donald Trump started talking about foreign trade, I have thought that what the country needs is a clear, easily understood book that explains why the government should not mess with free trade. Lo and behold, Ray Keating has written exactly that book. *Free Trade Rocks!* clears away the myths and misconceptions that trade interventionists count on."

- George Leef,
Director of Research,
James G. Martin Center for Academic Renewal

FREE TRADE ROCKS!

10 Points on International Trade Everyone Should Know

Ray Keating

Copyright © 2019 by Raymond J. Keating

All rights reserved.

For more information:
Keating Reports, LLC
raykeating@keatingreports.com

ISBN-13: 9781688412453

Cover design by Ray Keating.

*For
Jonathan,
David
and
Beth*

Previous Books by Ray Keating

In the nonfiction arena...

A Discussion Guide for Ray Keating's Warrior Monk
(Second Edition, 2019)

The Realistic Optimist TO DO List & Calendar 2019 (2018)

*Unleashing Small Business Through IP:
The Role of Intellectual Property in Driving Entrepreneurship,
Innovation and Investment* (Revised and Updated Edition, 2016)

*Unleashing Small Business Through IP:
Protecting Intellectual Property, Driving Entrepreneurship*
(2013)

*Discussion Guide for Warrior Monk:
A Pastor Stephen Grant Novel* (2011)

"Chuck" vs. the Business World: Business Tips on TV (2011)

*U.S. by the Numbers:
What's Left, Right, and Wrong with America State by State* (2000)

*New York by the Numbers:
State and City in Perpetual Crisis* (1997)

D.C. by the Numbers: A State of Failure (1995)

In the fiction arena...

Deep Rough: A Pastor Stephen Grant Novel (2019)

Warrior Monk: A Pastor Stephen Grant Novel
(Second Edition, 2019)

Shifting Sands: A Pastor Stephen Grant Short Story (2018)

Heroes & Villains: A Pastor Stephen Grant Short Story (2018)

Reagan Country: A Pastor Stephen Grant Novel (2018)

Lionhearts: A Pastor Stephen Grant Novel (2017)

Wine Into Water: A Pastor Stephen Grant Novel (2016)

Murderer's Row: A Pastor Stephen Grant Novel (2015)

The River: A Pastor Stephen Grant Novel (2014)

*An Advent for Religious Liberty:
A Pastor Stephen Grant Novel* (2012)

Root of All Evil? A Pastor Stephen Grant Novel (2012)

Warrior Monk: A Pastor Stephen Grant Novel (2010)

"The most important single central fact about a free market is that no exchange takes place unless both parties benefit."

- Milton Friedman

"Part of the difficulty in accepting the good news about trade is in our words. We too often talk about trade while using the vocabulary of war. In war, for one side to win, the other must lose. But commerce is not warfare. Trade is an economic alliance that benefits both countries. There are no losers, only winners. And trade helps strengthen the free world."

- President Ronald Reagan

"Our free trade plan is quite simple. We say that every Englishman shall have the right to buy whatever he wants, wherever he chooses, at his own good pleasure, without restriction or discouragement from the State. That is our plan."

- Winston Churchill

"Free trade is not based on utility but on justice."

- Edmund Burke

"Nothing ... can be more absurd than this whole doctrine of the balance of trade..."

- Adam Smith

Table of Contents

Introduction	1
Point 1: Do People "Get It" on Free Trade?	5
Point 2: Economics 101 on Trade	12
Point 3: Debunking Trade Myths	17
Point 4: Trade and the U.S. Economy	31
Point 5: Trading Partners	35
Point 6: Trade and Small Business	37
Point 7: Ills of Protectionism	40
Point 8: Brief History of Free Trade Deals	50
Point 9: The Morality of Free Trade	55
Point 10: The Future of Trade	59

Introduction

As an economist, let me make a couple of things clear when it comes to international trade. First, protectionism sucks. Second, free trade rocks. I know – not exactly highly technical stuff from the economics profession. But both points are true. So, let's get started backing up these bold claims.

We'll start by talking taxes. Most politicians understand that people don't like to pay taxes. However, many folks don't seem to get all that bothered when someone else gets hit with a bigger tax bill. There's an old ditty that dates back to the early 1930s that goes, "Don't tax you. Don't tax me. Tax the guy behind the tree."

It's pretty standard fare for politicians to push the idea of taxing others – especially higher taxes on high-income earners or the "rich" – in order to then promise government goodies for everybody else presumably paid for with the resulting additional revenues. It's class warfare, and it happens to be lousy economics.

Another group sometimes targeted for higher taxes is foreigners. Indeed, higher taxes can become an even easier sell if they are called tariffs – that is, taxes on imports – and politicians mistakenly or misleadingly argue that other countries wind up paying those tariffs.

While higher tariffs have popped up here and there during the post-World-War-II period, they largely were exceptions in a long-run move toward lower tariffs and freer trade. Both politicians and the public seemed to recall the role that high tariffs played in igniting the Great Depression (more on this later). But, of course, in politics, lessons eventually get unlearned.

The first glimmers of tariffs making a serious comeback arrived via the losing presidential efforts of Pat Buchanan and Ross Perot in the 1990s – Buchanan in 1992, 1996 and 2000, and Perot in 1992 and 1996. Later, during his 2008 presidential campaign, Barack Obama struck a hostile tone toward free trade, and then in 2016, Donald Trump made protectionism a centerpiece of his run for the White House.

Unlike Obama, who largely backed off his anti-trade campaign rhetoric after taking office, President Trump did the exact opposite. He pushed protectionist measures with an array of U.S. trading partners, including Mexico, Canada, China, South Korea, and Japan. One selling point by President Trump as he ramped up a trade war with China was that China, or Chinese businesses, would pay the tariffs he was imposing, not U.S. consumers or businesses.

In reality, the cost of higher taxes always spreads well beyond the groups targeted. For example, increased taxes on upper-income earners have negative effects on the private investment that is essential for economic, income and job growth. So, lots of people and the economy tend to suffer as resources are siphoned away from productive, private enterprises, and handed over to elected officials who dole out resources according to political incentives. As for tariffs on goods from China, for example, they wind up being paid by U.S. consumers and businesses who face increased costs and reduced choices.

There is the added political factor that consumers, at least, tend not to see the direct impact of tariffs clearly. In that way, tariffs are like regulations imposed by government. The effects are significant, but they are dealt with by others, such as by the businesses that must wrestle directly with increased costs. Compare these more-hidden costs to when government takes money directly out people's paychecks via an income tax increase, jacks up property tax bills, or hits consumers with higher sales taxes at the cash register. Workers and consumers – and yes, voters – see those costs quite clearly, and respond accordingly.

When it comes to tariffs, one might change that old-time ditty to: "Don't tax you. Don't tax me. Tax the guy across the sea." In reality, we all pay the price of higher tariffs in assorted ways.

But in getting at the basics of what free trade is, five fundamentals need to be summed up at the outset as to why free trade rocks!

First, and this obvious point is often missed, it's critical to keep in mind that governments, for the most part, do not trade; instead, individuals and businesses do. There's no difference between trades taking place across town, across the nation or around the globe. Trade happens between individuals, between businesses, and between individuals and businesses. Those trades would not occur if the parties involved were not made better off by such voluntary transactions. Trade, by definition, makes people better off.

Second, thanks to freer trade, competition is expanded and resources are allocated more efficiently, and therefore, consumers experience a wider choice of products and lower prices.

Third, entrepreneurs, businesses and workers experience greater opportunity with freer trade, as more markets are open to their goods and services.

Fourth, as individuals and businesses specialize in those areas where they have a comparative advantage – that is, their largest advantage – and then trade with others, economic, productivity and income growth are boosted.

Fifth, international trade is increasingly important for the U.S. economy and to U.S. economic growth. Again, we'll explore this more in an upcoming chapter, but for now, it's simply worth noting that in 1955, real total trade (that is, exports plus imports) equaled only 6.3 percent of U.S. GDP. As of 2018, total trade had risen to 32.3 percent of the economy.

To sum up, free trade reduces costs through enhanced competition and lower trade barriers; expands choices and lowers prices for consumers; keeps U.S. firms competitive; opens new markets and opportunities for U.S. goods and services; expands economic freedom; and feeds economic growth.

In the following pages, the benefits of free trade and the costs of protectionism – such as increased tariffs – hopefully will be clarified. And by doing so, we'll come to see more clearly that protectionism sucks, and free trade rocks!

Point 1: Do People "Get It" on Free Trade?

Free trade shouldn't be considered an economic mystery. Nor should it be viewed as something that benefits the few at the expense of the many. It also isn't about big business over small business, nor shareholders vs. workers. Finally, free trade is not about foreigners squaring off against or taking advantage of Americans.

In reality, free trade simply means reducing or eliminating the barriers and burdens placed on international trade by government. By providing such relief from the costs imposed by government – such as tariffs or quotas (i.e., limits placed on imports) – individuals and businesses experience greater freedom to produce, buy and sell goods and services. Consumers see greater choices and lower prices. In the end, free trade is about expanding opportunities.

But how many people fully "get it" on what free trade is, and what free trade actually means for consumers, businesses, workers, taxpayers and our economy? As an economist and columnist who has worked, written, and taught on international trade for some three decades, I sometimes worry that the numbers who truly grasp the basics of free trade are disturbingly small.

While free trade ranks as one of the very few issues where economists are overwhelmingly in agreement – and have been for a very long time – free trade faces differing views and swings in opinion among assorted other groups.

With noteworthy exceptions, of course, I've learned over the years that too many politicians can be a bit dim on economic matters, and that most certainly includes trade. Elected officials often fail to grasp how trade works, or they choose to put aside sound economics in favor of perceived political advantages.

For example, we'll delve in a bit more as to where the two major U.S. political parties stand on trade, but for now, suffice it to say that Democrats, for the most part in recent decades, have chosen to reject free trade. In response to strong political support from environmentalists and labor unions, Democrats have tended to favor using trade agreements to impose on other nations various environmental and labor regulations advocated by these supporters. Again, free trade is not about adding governmental costs, but instead, about reducing such burdens.

Meanwhile, Republicans tended to be more supportive of free trade than Democrats – particularly from the time of President Ronald Reagan through the administration of President George W. Bush. However, that changed notably with President Donald Trump. There seemed to be only one issue where Trump remained consistent over any extended period of time – from the 1980s to his time in the White House – and that was his opposition to free trade. As a candidate and as president (so far, as of this writing), Trump used populist rhetoric to stir up opposition to free trade. It remains unclear where the Republican Party might end up on trade during the post-Trump years.

As for the public's take on trade matters, polls point to views varying according to when the questions were asked, and what specifically was being asked. Let's now walk through an assortment of polling results on trade to hopefully better understand what the public gets and doesn't get on trade.

Consider, for example, the results of a Gallup poll taken in February 2019 and published on the organization's website. Americans largely recognized the benefits of U.S. trade with other countries in an assortment of areas. When asked if U.S. trade with other countries has a "mostly positive" or "mostly negative" effect in certain areas of the economy, the responses for "mostly positive" were 70 percent on "innovation and the development of new products," 67 percent on "U.S. economic growth," 63 percent on the "prices Americans pay for products," 61 percent for "American business," and 58 percent on the "quality of products." The least positive tally came regarding "jobs for U.S. workers," which came in at 51 percent saying "mostly positive" and 42 percent "mostly negative." None of the other issues asked about earned more than 35 percent for "mostly negative."

As noted in the chart below (from "Slim Majority in U.S. See Trade as Benefiting American Workers" by Jeffrey M. Jones, Gallup.com, March 21, 2019), a larger percentage of American saw foreign trade more as a threat to the economy as opposed to an opportunity for growth from 2005 to 2012, that is, during the period heading into and during the Great Recession (with support bottoming out in the midst of the recession) and for some three-plus years afterward.

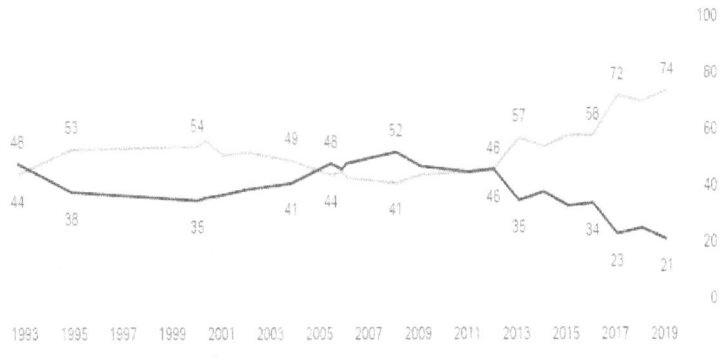

However, from 2013 into 2019, Americans increasingly saw foreign trade more as an opportunity for growth, with that view reaching record high levels in Gallup polling.

Interestingly, other polling on trade issues during the first half of 2019 also showed positive views on trade and concerns regarding tariffs.

For example, a Quinnipiac University poll of registered voters (May 16-20, 2019) found that 48 percent viewed President Trump's trade policies as "bad for the U.S. economy," while 40 percent viewed them as "good."

Among the findings in a Monmouth University poll (May 16-20, 2019) of adults, 51 percent viewed "free trade agreements with other countries" as "good" for the U.S., with only 14 percent saying "bad" and 29 percent being "unsure."

Of course, there are matters of consistency, or lack thereof, among some respondents. The Monmouth poll, for example, asked, "In general, do you think that imposing tariffs on products imported from other countries is good or bad for the United States, or are you not sure?" The responses were 37 percent "bad," 32 percent "good," and 23 percent "unsure." If consistent with the questions regarding free trade agreements, one would expect a higher percentage of respondents saying "bad" on tariffs and smaller share saying "good." Still, though, the overall leanings in favor of free trade and against government placing burdens on trade are clear – for now, at least.

A Pew Research poll on trade revealed even greater conflict in Americans' thinking or understanding on international trade. On the broad question of trade being good or bad for the United States, 74 percent said "good" and only 21 percent said "bad." However, getting into specifics, the optimism on international trade faded. On jobs, 36 percent agreed that trade with other countries creates jobs, with 34 percent saying jobs are destroyed and 24 percent saying trade makes no difference. On wages, 31 percent agreed that trade increases wages, 31 percent said trade reduces wages, and 30 percent said no difference. Finally, while 37 percent agreed that trade reduces prices, 32 percent said prices increase, and 25 percent said no difference.

However, contradiction reigned in an August 2018 MorningConsult/Politico poll. First, 42 percent of voters viewed free trade agreements as being positive for the U.S., compared 26 percent saying negative. But the same poll found that 48 percent of voters generally supported tariffs on goods also made in the United States, with 32 percent opposing such levies. Hmmm.

And then there is the impact of politics. As reported in July 2018, a Pew Research poll of American adults found: "Overall, nearly half (49%) of U.S. adults say increased tariffs between the U.S. and its trading partners will be bad for the country. A smaller share (40%) say the tariffs will be good for the U.S., while 11% say they don't know how the tariffs will affect the country." Digging deeper, though, this poll pointed to positions on tariffs being driven by political party affiliation. In recent history, at least, Republicans tended to favor free trade while Democrats were protectionist. But regarding President Trump's tariff efforts, Pew reported the following: "The survey, conducted July 11-15 among 1,007 adults, finds that attitudes toward the tariffs are deeply polarized. About seven-in-ten (73%) Republicans and Republican-leaning independents say increased tariffs between the U.S. and its trading partners will be a good thing for the country. Roughly the same share of Democrats and Democratic leaners (77%) say the increased tariffs will be a bad thing for the U.S."

Also in July 2018, Gallup found the party factor coming into play as well. As for the long-run effects of tariffs being imposed and debated at the time, for example, 62% of Republicans said that these tariffs would aid the U.S. economy, with 18% saying no difference and 17% saying the tariffs would make things worse. Meanwhile, only 12% of Democrats agreed that these tariffs would make things better, 14% saying not much difference, and 72% saying they would make matters worse.

And as for the state of the economy playing a part in the public's take on trade, if we go back to mid-November 2010, with the recession officially over but Americans still hurting and feeling as if the economy was still in recession, a poll released by Rasmussen Reports found that 40% of adults said free trade was good for the economy, with 26% saying it was bad and another 34% not sure. As for the impact of free trade on jobs specifically, 45% said it costs jobs, 26% said free trade creates jobs, and 27% were not sure.

Again, politics, and economic circumstances at the time matter when assessing Americans' views on trade. Yes, Americans seem conflicted or confused on how international trade affects the economy.

Yet, as already pointed out, international trade is one of the few areas where little disagreement exists among economists. Consider the following summary on the matter from Matthew Fienup ("Economists Do Agree on Something!" Center for Economic Research & Forecasting, California Lutheran University, March 29, 2018):

> In a 2009 survey by the American Institute of Economic Research, 83 percent of economists agreed that the U.S. should "eliminate remaining tariffs and other barriers to trade." Only 9.8 percent disagreed. Since 2009, the numbers have been even more one sided. In a 2012 survey of economists by the University of Chicago, 98 percent of respondents agreed that Americans are better off as a result of the North American Free Trade Agreement (NAFTA). In the University's October 2016 survey, 100 percent of respondents agreed that a plan to levy import tariffs in order to increase U.S. production is a bad idea... In the March 2018 survey, 100 percent of respondents stated that U.S. tariffs on steel and aluminum will not improve Americans' welfare.

Free Trade Rocks!

For good measure, N. Gregory Mankiw, a Harvard economist and former economic adviser to President George W. Bush, noted in a March 2008 *New York Times* article: "A 2006 poll of Ph.D. members of the American Economic Association found that 87.5 percent agreed that 'the U.S. should eliminate remaining tariffs and other barriers to trade.'" And William Poole noted in a 2004 article for the Federal Reserve Bank of St. Louis that more than 90 percent of U.S. economists in a 1990 survey agreed that tariffs and import quotas reduced the average standard of living.

Unfortunately, though, this agreement doesn't mean that economists necessarily have done a good job at communicating why free trade works or, for that matter, rocks. Indeed, it must be noted that at the time of the most recent polls of the public highlighted above, the U.S. had been in a long period of economic growth and the job market was relatively tight, so therefore, a more positive take on trade is not unexpected. Again, compare the 41 percent of adults saying trade was an opportunity for growth in 2008, according to Gallup, versus 72 percent in 2019. Did that change reflect a more in-depth understanding among the public on trade, or just a shift in economic conditions? I'd like to think that our knowledge of trade expanded in reach and depth, but hey, I have my doubts. In addition, the consistently high disapproval ratings for President Trump could indicate that political preferences played a role in driving up support for foreign trade during 2017-2019, given Trump's opposition.

So, what do we take away from these various polling numbers? In a nutshell, the American public tends to support freer trade as a general concept, but that support varies widely depending upon the particular focus of the question, the state of the economy when asked, and the politics at the time. That indicates support for free trade rests on a somewhat shaky foundation.

So, let's work to solidify thinking on trade, and make clear that, yeah, free trade rocks!

Point 2: Economics 101 on Trade

Yes, economists agree that free trade is a net economic plus. But they seem to face difficulties in communicating and teaching this fundamental economic lesson. That could be a failure on the part of economists, a lack of economics instruction in general, a willing ignorance among politicians and the public, and/or an assortment of these and other factors in the mix, such as how trade is reported in the media.

The average economics textbook does an adequate job of explaining the basics of trade. But there's obviously something missing. So, let's zero in on the two basic principles that largely explain what trade is all about, and take note of where those ideas on trade originated.

First, trade creates value. Quite simply, trade – or voluntary exchanges – between individuals, between individuals and businesses, and between businesses adds value. If that were not the case, then those trades would not occur. Again, this is the case whether transactions occur in the same town, within the same country, or across international borders.

Second, it follows then that individuals and businesses focus their energies and resources in areas where they have a comparative advantage, and trade with others accordingly. This is how local, national and international markets work, and work to benefit people. Specialization, division of labor and trade create value for all involved, adding to economic and income growth.

Free Trade Rocks! 13

Hold on. What's the deal with "comparative advantage," "specialization," and "division of labor"? Let's turn first to the big guy in economics – Adam Smith.

Smith was the eighteenth-century father of modern economics who, among other achievements, made historic strides in establishing the benefits of free trade. His contribution to economics, including why free trade makes sense, was his landmark book *An Inquiry into the Nature and Causes of the Wealth of Nations,* published in 1776.

Smith made the case "that trade which, without force or constraint, is naturally and regularly carried on between any two places, is always advantageous, though not always equally so, to both."

Ultimately, Smith made the case for free trade based on the concept of "absolute advantage." He wrote:

> It is the maxim of every prudent master of a family, never to attempt to make at home what it will cost him more to make than to buy. The tailor does not attempt to make his own shoes, but buys them of the shoemaker. The shoemaker does not attempt to make his own clothes, but employs a tailor. The farmer attempts to make neither the one nor the other, but employs those different artificers. All of them find it for their interest to employ their whole industry in a way in which they have some advantage over their neighbors, and to purchase with a part of its produce, or what is the same thing, with the price of a part of it, whatever else they have occasion for. What is prudence in the conduct of every private family can scarce be folly in that of a great kingdom. If a foreign country can supply us with a commodity cheaper than we ourselves can make it, better buy it from them with some part of the produce of our own industry, employed in a way in which we have some advantage.

Economist David Ricardo followed on Smith's heels in the early 19th century, moving beyond "absolute advantage" as justification for unencumbered international trade to "comparative advantage."

Comparative advantage merely shows that individuals and businesses prosper by producing the goods and services they are most efficient at producing, and then trading to acquire the other goods and services they need and want. Even if one holds an absolute advantage in a variety of areas, focusing on the endeavor where comparative advantage exists (i.e., where efficiency is maximized) and then trading with others creates a scenario where all prosper.

There are many examples illustrating the concept of comparative advantage, such as the doctor who may not only be a great heart surgeon but also an excellent office manager. In fact, this heart surgeon may hold an absolute advantage over his staff in terms of both surgery and office operations. However, the doctor will still hire and keep office staff because he holds a comparative advantage in surgery. The doctor prospers, as does his staff.

So, while comparative advantage is used to illustrate the mutual benefits from international trade, it, of course, holds for all markets and market transactions.

Meanwhile, "division of labor" explains the separation of tasks into a variety of related operations. Individuals are able to specialize in certain areas, and through such specialization become more productive. Trade promotes and enhances the benefits of division and specialization of labor. For good measure, through enhanced competition and cooperation, investment and innovation are driven forward, resulting in new and improved products, technologies, processes, and techniques. Quite simply, trade allows people to specialize, become more productive, enhance their incomes, and have access to goods and services far beyond anything that could be accomplished without trade.

I firmly believe that one of the great obstacles to non-economists understanding how trade works is the language of trade. From the days of Smith and Ricardo to economists today, while most economists have gotten the economics of trade correct, most have gotten the language of trade wrong. That is, the economics profession has done a disservice by talking about trade occurring between countries. For example, the language of the United States trading with Mexico or Canada or China again is misleading, and it often sets up an us-vs.-them perspective among non-economists.

This is further fed by how trade numbers are reported. We are treated each month to aggregate data on trade between nations, including the balance of trade (more on that later). This feeds the us-vs.-them mentality on trade. In an article ("International Trade") in *The Concise Encyclopedia of Economics*, Arnold Kling made the point that us-vs.-them notions are more akin to sports rather than economics. He wrote:

> For most people, viewing trade as a rivalry is as instinctive as rooting for their national team in Olympic basketball.
>
> To economists, Olympic basketball is *not* an appropriate analogy for international trade. Instead, we see international trade as analogous to a production technique. Opening up to trade is equivalent to adopting a more efficient technology.

The language of trade needs to change to reflect the reality that it is not nations trading with nations. Instead, the language of trade needs to be clarified so as to make clear that international trade is about individuals and businesses buying and selling goods and services with other individuals and businesses in other countries.

The same goes for how trade numbers are reported. Indeed, it will be noted in the next chapter that certain trade data reported by government are so misleading that perhaps they should not even be published.

The weaknesses in the language used and numbers reported on trade wind up feeding an array of myths that have come to dominate much of our public talk and action on international trade.

We need to debunk such myths in order to make clear that free trade rocks.

Point 3: Debunking Trade Myths

Myths about the economy and how it works seem to spread everywhere – in politics, the media, in business, and in the voting booth. But the subject of international trade might be hampered by more myths – or untruths – than any other area of our economy.

We're going to engage in quick myth-debunking in four areas.

Myth #1: Imports are Bad

The widespread assumption is that imports rank as economic negatives. An anti-imports bias certainly exists when trade numbers are reported in the media.

But isn't that the case? After all, consider how trade is treated when measuring gross domestic product (GDP), which is the total market value of all final goods and services produced in an economy. The change in real (inflation-adjusted) GDP is a key measure of economic growth and well-being. When you look at GDP data, it is clearly stated in the tables that imports are subtracted from exports to arrive at net exports. Net exports are added to personal consumption expenditures, gross private domestic investment, and government purchases to arrive at total GDP. Therefore, increasing imports means lower net exports, and therefore, lower GDP – right? Actually, no.

Imports are subtracted from GDP not because they are somehow negatives for the economy and growth. They are subtracted to avoid distorting GDP numbers.

It must be understood that the consumption numbers in GDP include consumption of imported goods and services. As for the GDP measure of investment, again, it includes both domestic and foreign capital or intermediate goods. And the same goes for government consumption and investment. Even when it comes to exports, those products can be made with goods that were imported.

Quite simply, imports are already counted in these other GDP measures. If imports were not then subtracted, GDP would be overstated. And since gross *domestic* product is about *domestic* production, imports do not directly affect GDP.

What about other ways that imports convey information about the economy or indirectly affect growth?

First, the early nineteenth century French economist Jean-Baptiste Say reminded us that "products are always bought ultimately with products." This is known as "Say's Law." It makes clear that in a market economy, one must produce marketable goods or services in order to be able to purchase goods or services, including imports. In essence, expanding imports correspond with expanding domestic production. During good economic times, individuals and families purchase more consumer goods, including imports, and businesses are expanding investment, including the purchase of imported capital goods (i.e., goods used to make other goods) or intermediate goods.

Second, imports aid the economy by boosting competition. Increased competition from imports pushes domestic producers to be more efficient and innovative. That's a key point against protectionism and in favor of free trade.

Third, due to enhanced competition, efficiency and innovation, consumers wind up with increased choices and lower prices. Those lower prices free up resources for saving, investing and making other purchases. So, the impact that imports have on competition and prices flow into enhanced income and faster economic growth.

Assorted reporters and talking heads then could not be more wrong about what imports mean to the economy. Imports do not subtract from the economy. Quite the contrary, imports both reflect what's occurring in and provide a boost to the overall economy.

In May 2013, a helpful report titled "Imports Work for America" was published by four business groups – the U.S. Chamber of Commerce, the Consumer Electronics Association, the National Retail Federation, and the American Apparel and Footwear Association. A key point from the report: "This study measures the many positive effects of merchandise imports on the U.S. economy, from employment-creation and U.S. manufacturing competitiveness — two factors commonly thought to suffer ill effects from imports — to a higher U.S. standard of living and wider consumer choice. On balance, the net impact of imports on the U.S. economy and on U.S. jobs is positive."

Again, while strange to many, that conclusion lines up with sound economic thinking.

After all, as already pointed out, trade creates value. The situation of each party involved in any trade is improved, otherwise a trade would not occur. And the fact that a trade occurs within a nation or across country borders matters not. In that report, the fundamental concept of comparative advantage was summed up, "As individuals and as an economy, Americans will always earn more by doing what we do best, and letting others with talents, skills and resources in other areas do what they do best."

"Imports Work for America" highlighted five critical points to keep in mind on imports.

First, U.S. consumers benefit from expanded choice and lower prices. As pointed out: "Imports expand selection of budget-friendly goods, like electronics we use to communicate and many clothes and shoes we wear, and improve the year-round supply of such staples as fresh fruits and vegetables."

Second, contrary to popular opinion, imports are a net plus – not a minus – for U.S. jobs. It was found that in 2011, "U.S. imports supported more than 16 million *net*, direct and indirect American jobs, representing 9.3 percent of total U.S. employment." Those jobs come from enhanced spending power of American families and businesses, and increased economic activity tied to imports.

Third, importing is big business for small businesses. It turns out that more than half of U.S. importers have less than 50 employees. (More on this later in this book.)

Fourth, imports make U.S. manufacturers and farmers more competitive, as they use imported inputs to reduce costs. In fact, capital goods, and industrial supplies and materials accounted for more than 61 percent of U.S. goods imports in 2012.

Finally, it turns out that imports help generate exports. As explained in the report, "The United States is integrated into an international supply chain that means that even U.S. imports contain U.S. exports – R&D, design, and inputs that were exported for further manufacture abroad."

Looking at imports as part of GDP, a proper understanding of how the economy is measured makes clear that imports do not subtract from the U.S. economy. And more fundamentally, Jean-Baptiste Say's lesson that "products are always bought ultimately with products" makes clear that growing imports must correspond with expanding domestic production.

Myth #2: Trade Deficits are Bad

Given the pervasiveness of the imports-are-bad myth, it's not surprising – indeed, it follows – that most people would buy into the myth that trade deficits (imports exceeding exports in trade between particular nations or with all other trading partners) are negative signals or indicators on the economy.

The emphasis on trade deficits is a return to the pre-Adam Smith days when mercantilism held sway over thinking about trade. Mercantilism? In summary, mercantilism called for protectionist measures that encouraged exports and discouraged imports so that a nation could accrue large reserves of gold and silver. The balance of trade mattered most to the mercantilists.

Today's emphasis on the "balance of trade" is a form of modern-day mercantilism, and it again can be seen in the media, in political circles, and among too many economists. President Trump, for example, ranks as a modern-day mercantilist, claiming that running a trade deficit means that the U.S. is somehow losing.

The problem is that mercantilism, whether in the 18th century or today, assumes that no mutual benefits exist in trading, in particular, when individuals and businesses trade across borders. Mercantilists see international trade in terms of somebody winning and somebody losing in a kind of zero-sum game. But that, of course, is not how trade actually works. Trade occurs between individuals, between businesses, and between individuals and businesses, across towns, nations and international borders. And a voluntary, market trade is mutually beneficial, otherwise it would not occur.

Smith's arguments began the dismantling of any intellectual legitimacy mercantilism might claim. For example, on the balance of trade, Smith noted:

> Nothing, however, can be more absurd than this whole doctrine of the balance of trade, upon which, not only these restraints, but almost all other regulations of commerce are founded. When two places trade with one another, this doctrine supposes that if the balance be even neither of them either loses or gains; but if it leans in any degree to one side, that one of them loses, and the other gains in proportion to its declension from the exact equilibrium. Both suppositions are false... But that trade which, without force or constraint, is naturally and

regularly carried on between any two places, is always advantageous, though not always equally so, to both.

Later, Smith observed: "Every town and country ... in proportion as they have opened their ports to all nations, instead of being ruined by this free trade, ... have been enriched by it."

Let's get a few basic trade principles clear.

A country's balance of payments sums up transactions of individuals, businesses and government with foreigners. And there are three accounts in the mix.

First, the *current* account is about trade in goods and services, as well as smaller items, namely, income from investments and unilateral transfers, or gifts. The U.S. usually runs a current account deficit, due to a deficit in the trade of goods and services.

Second is the *capital* account, which sums up changes in ownership, that is, ownership in real and financial assets, and it includes direct investments and loans. The U.S. runs a capital account surplus, that is, capital inflows to the U.S. exceed capital outflows. People like to invest here.

Third, the *official reserve* account consists of transactions by governments in foreign exchange markets. Given the U.S. dollar's unofficial role of the world's reserve currency, foreign governments often hold U.S. Treasury bonds, for example.

In the end, the balance of payments accounts must, well, balance. That is, the current account balance plus the capital account balance plus the official reserve account balance will equal zero.

So, what does all of this mean in terms of trade?

The U.S. runs a capital account surplus because it's an attractive place to invest, which is great since such investment helps to fuel economic, productivity, income and job growth. In turn, the U.S. will run a current account deficit, including a trade deficit. Once more, contrary to the assumptions of too many politicians, that's not bad news.

Free Trade Rocks! 23

Rather, it again points to the positives in the American economy.

The history of trade deficits also must be noted. Throughout much of U.S. history, periods of higher economic growth tended to coincide with shrinking trade surpluses or mounting trade deficits.

For example, looking at recent history, the U.S. trade deficit shrank dramatically during the most recent recession (late 2007 to mid-2009). The deficit also declined during the poor economy of 1990-91. And during the economic woes of 1979 to 1982, the trade deficit again declined notably, even moving to a trade surplus for two of those years.

In contrast, periods of solid growth have seen the trade deficit expand, such as during 1982 to 1986, 1996 to 2000, and 2002 to 2006.

Again, this is not necessarily surprising given what we've noted about the balance of payments.

A May 2019 report ("Historical U.S. Trade Deficits") from the Federal Reserve Bank of St. Louis made clear that trade deficits are not economic negatives. While there are problems with this analysis – including falling prey to mistakenly asserting or indicating that, in effect, nations trade with other nations – the authors hit on some basic points that need to be kept in mind regarding trade deficits, such as:

- "Running a trade deficit is nothing new for the United States. Indeed, it has run a persistent trade deficit since the 1970s—but it also did throughout most of the 19th century."

- "From 1800-1870, the United States ran a trade deficit for all but three years and the trade balance averaged about –2.2 percent of GDP. Then from 1870-1970, it ran persistent trade surpluses that averaged about 1.1 percent of GDP. Starting in about 1970, the United States began to run trade deficits again, which have continued to this day."

• During the 19th century, "Since countries trade based on their comparative advantages, we would expect to see long-term changes to a country's trade as it enters a new stage of development. U.S. consumers benefited from imported manufactured goods, and furthermore, the United States could import capital goods to facilitate its own industrialization."

• "The United States ran persistent trade deficits for large parts of its history, just as it does today. Trade deficits did not inhibit U.S. development, however, and may have even facilitated industrialization as the United States could import capital goods to improve its own manufacturing during its first phase of industrialization."

Finally, in a March 2018 *Washington Times* column titled "Destructive Information," economist Richard Rahn explained why the trade deficit basically is irrelevant:

> There is some information that the government should never publish because it is so little understood by the political class and the media. A prime example is the trade deficit number. The trade deficit is of little importance, but as we now see, a focus on that number is causing the president and others to impose destructive tariffs and other harmful trade restrictions. The trade deficit, which is officially known as the "current account balance," is merely the residual of many other policies by both the U.S. and foreign governments.

Rahn looked at data for 13 countries, and reported that "there is no obvious relationship between a country's trade deficit, level of prosperity, growth in GDP per capita or tariff rate." He clarified, "Some rich jurisdictions, like Singapore, Switzerland and Hong Kong, have zero tariffs (free trade) and run large trade surpluses. Some high-tariff countries, like Mexico, have run trade deficits, while having had low growth rates, coupled with a low per capita income. China has had a very high rate of per capita economic growth over the last 25 years, and high tariff rates, but still has a relatively low per capita income. Japan and Italy have had relatively low tariff rates, and low growth, but substantial trade surpluses. Italy and Ireland have had the same relatively low average tariff rate (both being members of the European Union), and both run trade surpluses."

Rahn also noted: "The U.S. government has been keeping foreign trade statistics since 1790. In the majority of years, the U.S. ran a trade deficit and an offsetting capital surplus (meaning more money was invested in the U.S. than U.S. companies and individuals invested in the rest of the world). The U.S., by productively using inexpensive foreign capital, was able to create the world's biggest and wealthiest economy."

In the end, Rahn is right – the trade deficit really does not matter. Instead, the direction on both exports and imports is what matters. That is, expanding exports mean expanding opportunities for U.S. businesses and workers, while growing imports reflect domestic growth and benefits thanks to increased competition, lower prices and costs, increased choices, and improved quality.

Myth #3: Devaluing the Dollar is Good for Trade

Lots of politicians, TV talking heads, and even some CEOs – usually heading up manufacturing firms – love pushing the idea that a declining dollar is good for U.S. industry and economic growth. They claim that a weaker dollar makes U.S. exports cheaper, and imports more expensive. I'm not sure why that would necessarily be good, but it's not really how it works in the end anyway.

First, one has to understand that as much as we talk about "floating exchange rates," this is a dirty float. That is, governments control the supply of their currencies, and often work to manipulate a currency's value. For example, politicians like U.S. Senator Charlie Schumer (D-NY) and President Donald Trump have complained about China manipulating its currency. But politicians and others serving up such complaints simply are looking for this other nation, like China, to manipulate its currency according to these politicians' preferences. (More on this in a moment.)

Second, monetary devaluation is not good news for industry and economic growth. With a weaker currency, it's clear that a nation is a less attractive place in which to invest. When devaluations are sudden, economies face tumult and crisis. And when weakening happens over a longer stretch of time, the country suffers a more gradual diminishment in investment and growth. Basically, devaluation reduces returns, and therefore, lessens incentives for investment. For example, consider that the value of the U.S. dollar versus other major currencies declined markedly from early 2002 to mid-late 2011, and that largely covered a period of slow growth and the Great Recession.

Third, the idea that exports become cheaper and imports more expensive eventually is undermined by arbitrage and price adjustments. At best, exporters can hope for a short-term gain, but again at the risk of larger economic woes. In addition, advocates for a weak dollar ignore the fact that it's not just consumer products that are imported, but also capital goods and inputs. That reality raises serious doubts even about any temporary, short-term benefits that might be hoped for with a weaker dollar for U.S. exporters.

Fourth, even to the extent that a devaluation takes hold, it's not beneficial for the country that is devaluing its currency. In a January 2017 report from George Mason

University's Mercatus Center, economist Donald J. Boudreaux and Nita Ghei ironically pointed out:

> So-called "currency manipulation" by a trading partner does not harm the American economy. For example, a lower price of the yuan makes Chinese goods cheaper for American consumers, conferring a real benefit on the United States. Keeping the price of the yuan lower through monetary policy, however, does not lower the real costs of the resources and outputs exported by the Chinese people, who also face higher prices for American imports. An undervalued yuan – assuming this undervaluation to be real rather than fanciful – benefits Americans at the expense of the Chinese.

Finally, currency fluctuations really matter little to the well-being of U.S. manufacturers when compared to economic growth. It's difficult to unearth a reliable pattern tying U.S. manufacturing production to fluctuations in the dollar. For example, manufacturing output grew robustly from late 1982 into 1989. But during that period, the value of the U.S. dollar experienced a dramatic rise, and then a big fall off. Also, manufacturing grew from late 1993 to mid-2000, and the dollar rose over that same period.

Rather, the well-being of U.S. industry, including manufacturing, is about the state of economic growth – here and abroad. Looking at data since the early 1970s, U.S. manufacturing production has declined notably only during and around each recession.

Consider, again, the example of China. The U.S. has long had a trade deficit with China. In 2018, the U.S. deficit in goods and services trade with China was $380.8 billion. This deficit angers various politicians, who usually blame China's yuan exchange rate with the dollar. U.S politicians are good at accusing China of currency manipulation to keep the yuan's value low so as to promote exports and limit imports. How do politicians and their appointees know the yuan is undervalued? Well, apparently, they just do. After all, look at that trade deficit.

But no reason exists to think that exports and imports should balance between particular nations. Given the realities of our respective economies, Americans purchase lots of goods produced at lower cost in China, while far lower incomes among the Chinese mean they buy fewer goods we produce, such as in the high-tech arena. At the same time, though, China is the third largest goods export market for the U.S.

Also, since the U.S. ran trade surpluses with nations like Canada, Brazil, Hong Kong, Singapore, and the United Kingdom, as well as with South/Central America, in 2018, should those nations call on the U.S. to adjust the dollar to fit their political desires? That's exactly what the U.S. wants from China, however. U.S. politicians really aren't against China currency manipulation per se. Quite the contrary, they just want China to manipulate the yuan in a way deemed advantageous to the U.S.

But what about China allowing the yuan to float freely and letting market forces determine its value? This, once more, is the big fiction about exchange rates. Sure, currencies are traded, but no true free market in currencies exists because governments create money, and reduce or expand the supply of money according to policy desires. There's that "dirty float."

In the end, when the dollar is strong, it means that investors see the U.S. as a sound investment, a place of economic growth and low inflation.

Myth #4: Free Trade Means Lost Jobs and Lower Pay

The most widely asserted myth is that free trade means lost jobs and lost pay for Americans. The assertion basically is that low-wage foreign workers take away U.S. jobs. While particular jobs may be lost due to more open international

Free Trade Rocks!

trade, overall economic and income growth, as well as job creation, clearly are enhanced.

Consider three key problems with the lost-jobs-lower-pay assertions.

First, opponents of free trade essentially subscribe to a zero-sum view of the world. According to this view, only so many jobs exist to be divvied up among the masses. Of course, this is not the way the economy functions. Thanks to entrepreneurship, investment, innovation and trade, all disciplined by competition and consumer sovereignty, economies and incomes grow, wealth is created, and jobs are generated.

Second, as trade barriers and costs are reduced via free trade agreements, for example, specialization is enhanced, and workers become more productive. In addition, imports aid the economy by boosting competition, which drives domestic businesses to be more innovative and to further improve productivity. And it is productivity that serves as a key determinant of income, that is, in general, the greater the productivity, the higher the income level.

Third, free trade accords entered into by the United States overwhelmingly are about our trading partners reducing much higher trade barriers than the U.S. had imposed. Therefore, it is important to understand that these trade agreements do not provide added incentives to shift economic production from the U.S. to those nations. Instead, opportunities for U.S. businesses to export goods to those countries are enhanced.

It's also worth noting that export-related jobs pay more on average. The U.S. International Trade Commission has noted that "export-intensive industries pay more on average and that the export earnings premium is larger for blue collar workers in production and support occupations (they earn a 19.0% premium in export-intensive manufacturing industries and a 17.6% premium in export-intensive services industries) than for white collar workers in management and professional occupations (they earn a 9.9% premium in export-intensive manufacturing industries and a 12.0% premium in export-intensive services industries). Overall, the export earnings premium in 2014 is 16.3% on average in the manufacturing industries and 15.5% on average in the services industries."

So, contrary to prevailing myths, imports are not bad; trade deficits are not economic negatives; dollar devaluation makes no sense; and freer trade boosts productivity, and therefore, incomes. Yes, indeed, free trade rocks.

Point 4: Trade and the U.S. Economy

Trade is a bigger part of the U.S. economy than ever before, and therefore, trade is of increasing importance to U.S. businesses, workers and consumers.

Consider that in 1955, for example, U.S. real exports came in at 2.8 percent of real GDP. That grew to 6.0 percent in 1980, and to 13.6 percent in 2018.

Meanwhile, imports equaled 3.6 percent of the economy in 1955, rising to 6.0 percent in 1980 and 18.5 percent in 2018.

If we then look at total trade (exports plus imports), it equaled 6.3 percent of the economy in 1955, rising to 12 percent in 1980 and 32.1 percent in 2018.

Focusing on growth, from 1955 to 2018, real GDP grew at an annual average rate of 3.1 percent. Over the same period, trade grew at a far faster pace. Average annual growth in real exports registered 5.9 percent and real imports 6.0 percent. So, trade grew at almost double the rate of the overall economy.

And from 1980 to 2018, the growth in real exports accounted for 17.9 percent of real total economic growth, and the increase in total trade equaled 43.6 percent of GDP growth over that same period.

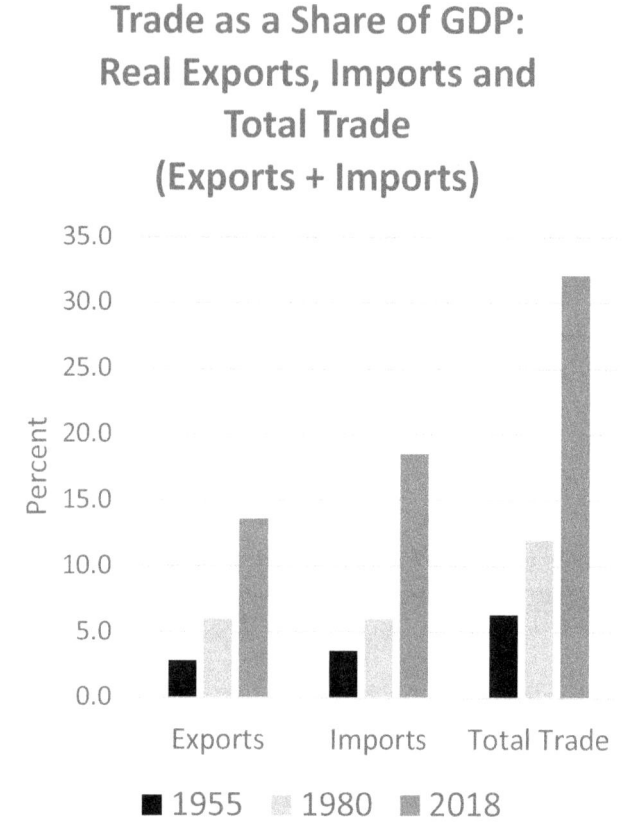

Data Source: U.S. Bureau of Economic Analysis

For good measure, when I talk trade with people, there seems to be a widespread assumption that the U.S. "doesn't make anything anymore" and the U.S. "doesn't export anything." Both assertions fail to jibe with economic reality.

First, U.S. industrial production – that is, stuff made in the U.S. such as through manufacturing and mining – has grown steadily over the past century. Even after a big drop in industrial production during the major recession that ran from late 2007 to mid-2009, and a subsequent under-performing recovery/expansion period, industrial production eventually climbed back and went on to hit new highs in the later half of 2014, and then again in 2018.

Of course, we've already noted that U.S. exports have been growing at a faster rate than the overall economy for some time. In addition, the U.S. ranks as the world's second largest merchandise exporter – again, understanding that businesses do the exporting, not a nation – with China ranking number one and Germany number three. After Germany, Japan runs at a distant fourth.

What does the U.S. export? WorldTopExports.com offered the following top 10 list of U.S. goods exports for 2018:

1. Machinery including computers: $213.1 billion
2. Mineral fuels including oil: $189.9 billion
3. Electrical machinery, equipment: $176.1 billion
4. Aircraft, spacecraft: $139.1 billion
5. Vehicles: $130.6 billion
6. Optical, technical, medical apparatus: $89.6 billion
7. Plastics, plastic articles: $66.5 billion
8. Gems, precious metals: $63.8 billion
9. Pharmaceuticals: $48.4 billion
10. Organic chemicals: $40.2 billion

U.S. farmers and ranchers also are major exporters on the agricultural front. The U.S. Department of Agriculture highlighted top U.S. agricultural exports in the chart on the next page.

The American Farm Bureau Federation has noted, "$139.6 billion worth of American agricultural products were exported around the world" in 2018, and about 25 percent of U.S. farm products are exported annually.

Regarding jobs, trade matters a great deal from a positive standpoint. As the Business Roundtable has reported ("How the U.S. Economy Benefits from International Trade and Investment"), international trade – both exports and imports – supports 41 million U.S. jobs.

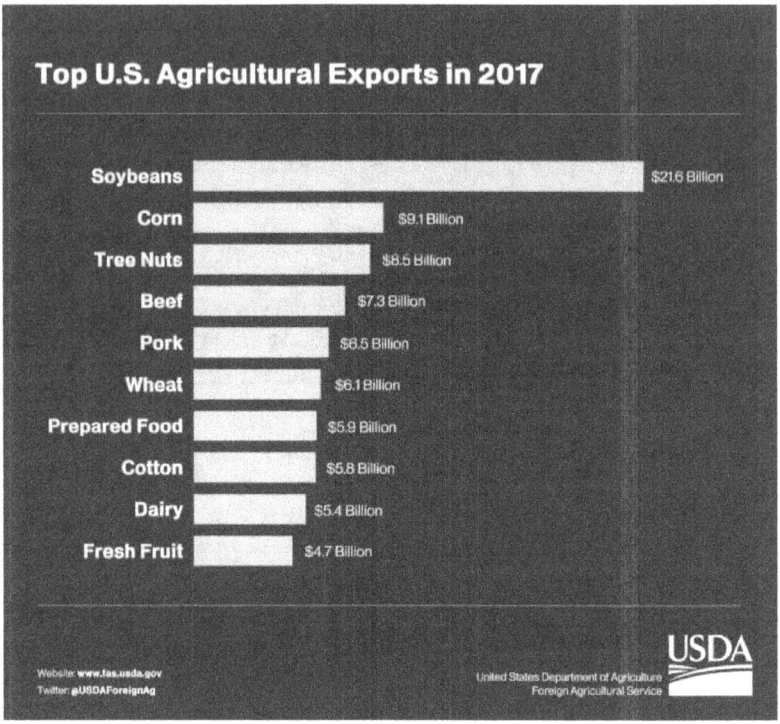

No matter how you slice it – growth in exports, imports and total trade; trade's share of the economy and economic growth; individual industries and their role in the global economy; or jobs; the U.S. is a trade powerhouse.

As for the overall impact of trade on the U.S. economy, consider that a May 2017 study by the Peterson Institute for International Economics found that the benefits to the United States from expanded trade – thanks to trade liberalization – from 1950 to 2016 amounted to $2.1 trillion (measured in 2016 dollars), with per capita GDP and GDP per household increasing by $7,014 and $18,131, respectively.

Therefore, reducing governmental barriers, and thereby expanding opportunities, via free trade accords is vital to the U.S. economy. Indeed, it should be clear, from the role and importance of trade in the U.S. economy and among so many industries, that free trade rocks!

Point 5: Trading Partners

The misleading language of trade comes into play when the subject of trading partners comes up. The rhetoric and the data promote the idea that countries trade with countries. For example, we hear a great deal about which countries are the top trading partners with the United States.

However, the reality again is that individuals and businesses trade with individuals and businesses, whether across town or across international borders. With that in mind, let's consider where U.S. businesses and consumers do the bulk of their international transactions.

The top nations in 2018 with which U.S. businesses and consumers traded were China, Canada and Mexico, with Japan coming in a distant fourth. See the following tables in terms of exports, imports and total trade:

Top Six Nations for U.S. Exports, 2018

Country	Exports in Billions$
Canada	$365.5
Mexico	$299.8
China	$178.0
United Kingdom	$140.8
Japan	$121.2
Germany	$92.4

Data Source: U.S. Bureau of Economic Analysis

Top Six Nations for U.S. Imports, 2018

Country	Imports in Billions$
China	$558.8
Mexico	$378.4
Canada	$360.9
Japan	$179.1
Germany	$159.8
United Kingdom	$122.1

Data Source: U.S. Bureau of Economic Analysis

Top Six Nations in U.S. Total Trade (Exports + Imports), 2018

Country	Total Trade in Billions$
China	$736.8
Canada	$726.4
Mexico	$678.2
Japan	$300.3
United Kingdom	$262.9
Germany	$252.2

Data Source: U.S. Bureau of Economic Analysis

So, these are the top nations with which American businesses and consumers generate the greatest value by engaging in trade. Again, voluntary trade going on between businesses and individuals across these borders by definition makes each side better off. As we see, once more, free trade rocks!

Point 6: Trade and Small Business

When talking about trade and business, more often than not, people seem to assume that international trade is almost exclusively the domain of large firms. Sure, trade is big business for the U.S., as we've seen, but it's also completely about big business, right? Well, no.

To the contrary, small business is a big player in international trade. In fact, the overwhelming majority of businesses involved in trade rank as small or medium-sized enterprises. The numbers actually are rather striking.

According to the latest U.S. Census Bureau data (for 2016), among U.S. exporters:

- 76.1 percent have fewer than 20 employees, and they produce 14.8 percent of export value;

- 86.6 percent have fewer than 50 workers, and they produce 18.2 percent of export value;

- 91.8 percent have fewer than 100 employees, and they produce 21.1 percent of export value;

- and 97.5 percent have fewer than 500 workers, and they produce 33.3 percent of export value.

And among U.S. importers:

- 76.1 percent have fewer than 20 employees, and they account for 14.1 percent of value among importers;

- 86.1 percent have fewer than 50 workers, and they account for 17.9 percent of value among importers;

- 91.3 percent have fewer than 100 employees, and they account for 21.5 percent of value among importers;

- and 97.3 percent have fewer than 500 workers, and they account for 32.3 percent of value among importers.

The role of small businesses in trade holds up when looking at U.S. trade with individual nations as well. Consider the nations that rank top three among U.S. trading partners.

China. Regarding U.S. exporters to China, 53.7 percent have fewer than 20 employees, 68.7 percent have fewer than 50 employees, 78.4 percent have fewer than 100 workers, and 92.1 percent have fewer than 500 employees.

As for importers dealing with China, 74.3 percent have fewer than 20 employees, 84.9 percent have fewer than 50, 90.2 percent have fewer than 100, and 96.7 percent have fewer than 500 employees.

Canada. Looking at trade with Canada, 59.9 percent of U.S. exporters have fewer than 20 employees, 75.3 percent have fewer than 50 employees, 83.7 percent have fewer than 100 workers, and 94.4 percent have fewer than 500.

Meanwhile, 43.3 percent of importers have fewer than 20 employees, 55.7 percent have fewer than 50 employees, 65.3 percent have fewer than 100, and 83.0 percent have fewer than 500 workers.

Mexico. And among U.S. exporters to Mexico, 57.7 percent have fewer than 20 workers, 72.3 percent have fewer than 50 employees, 81.4 percent have fewer than 100, and 93.6 percent have fewer than 500 workers.

Regarding importing from Mexico, 57.6 percent have fewer than 20 workers, 67.9 percent have fewer than 50 employees, 74.6 percent have fewer than 100, and 86.8 percent have fewer than 500 employees.

International trade very much is a small business story. Therefore, whether we're talking about large, mid-size or small businesses, free trade rocks!

Point 7:
Ills of Protectionism

Protectionism is the exact opposite of free trade. It often gets dressed up in nice rhetoric, like "fair trade." But protectionism simply is the imposition of government barriers and obstacles on international trade, usually to please some special interest seeking political protection from competition. These trade barriers include tariffs (or taxes on imports); quotas (or limits on certain imports); rules and regulations imposed to discourage foreign businesses from doing business in the country; and the devaluing of currency in a futile attempt to boost exports and reduce imports.

For example, U.S. steel makers often seek to impose higher tariffs on imported steel. And U.S. sugar growers work the political system to limit sugar imports. Indeed, both industries have been pursuing such special favors from government for decades – the steel industry since the late 1960s and sugar since the 1930s.

Let's get at what the actual effects of protectionism are.

First, via tariffs, quotas and/or assorted rules and regulations, protectionism raises prices and limits choices for U.S. consumers. If you want to pay more for goods and have fewer options, then protectionism is for you.

Second, protectionism shields companies from competition – thereby reducing efficiency and quality, and limiting innovation.

Third, protectionism reduces international opportunities for U.S. entrepreneurs, businesses and workers as other nations retaliate, resulting in slower economic growth and fewer jobs.

Fourth, protectionism hurts U.S. businesses and workers who also pay more for whatever product is being shielded from competition.

For example, as Daniel Hannan wrote in the Foreword to *Traders of the Lost Ark: Rediscovering a Moral and Economic Case for Free Trade*: "There are, depending on how we do the counting, between 80,000 and 150,000 people working in the American steel industry. But there are 17 million people employed in sectors that use steel, notably construction, manufacturing, and cars."

And more businesses and workers use sugar than produce sugar. As reported in an April 2018 analysis of the U.S. sugar program by the Cato Institute ("Candy-Coated Cartel: Time to Kill the U.S. Sugar Program"), "Predictably, this approach has resulted in a steady stream of candy manufacturers shifting production to take advantage of cheaper sugar prices outside the country... A *Wall Street Journal* analysis of U.S. Census Bureau data found that total U.S. confectionary manufacturing employment declined by 22 percent from 1998 through 2011, while a 2006 Commerce Department study concluded that 'for each sugar growing and harvesting job saved through high U.S. sugar prices, nearly three confectionery manufacturing jobs are lost'; every sugar job saved was at a cost of $826,000."

It pays to take a brief journey further back in history to get a fuller story on the role played by tariffs. From the birth of the nation into the early 20th century, the U.S. federal government was relatively small and it was largely funded by revenues from tariffs. But for the Civil War and a brief period in the 1890s (1894 and 1895), Americans wisely avoided imposing income taxes. However, after the 16th Amendment to the U.S. Constitution allowing for an income tax was ratified in 1913, a federal personal income tax was imposed, and it served as high-octane fuel for the growth of government. The option of funding the federal government to any significant degree with tariffs disappeared.

Prior to the 16th Amendment, while tariffs were used primarily to fund the federal government, there were periodic bouts of using tariffs as instruments of protectionism as well.

While Alexander Hamilton, the first U.S. Treasury secretary, often is portrayed as a protectionist, that wasn't the case. His proposed, and largely implemented, tariff system was meant to pay off the public debt, as opposed to protecting certain industries. Hamilton needed imports as a tax base, so he did not favor high levels of tariffs that discouraged imports.

However, President Thomas Jefferson went in a very different and unique direction on trade. Douglas A. Irwin explained ("Historical Aspects of U.S. Trade Policy," National Bureau of Economic Research):

> Indeed, as president, Jefferson was responsible for one of the most unusual policy experiments in the history of U.S. trade policy. At his request, Congress imposed a nearly complete embargo on international commerce from December 1807 to March 1809... By mid-1808, the United States was about as close to being fully shut off from international commerce as it has ever been during peacetime.
>
> Monthly price data allow us to observe the dramatic impact of the embargo: the export-weighted average of the prices of raw cotton, flour, tobacco, and rice, which accounted for about two-thirds of U.S. exports in the United States, fell by one third within a month or two of the embargo. The price of imported commodities rose by about a third as the number of ships entering U.S. ports fell to a trickle and imports became increasingly scarce. According to my calculations, the static welfare cost of the

Free Trade Rocks! 43

embargo was about 5 percent of GDP. Thus, the embargo inflicted substantial costs on the economy during the short period that it was in effect.

Irwin also found that the embargo and the decline in trade thanks to the War of 1812 did not play any role promoting domestic manufacturing as the trend in growth in industrial production during that time was "little changed."

The next bout of protection came in the 1820s, in particular, the Tariff of 1828 – or as it has come to be known the Tariff of Abominations. Beyond its revenue purposes, politics brought together western and northern interests to push tariffs drastically higher. However, the results featured higher costs of living in the South and increased costs for New England businesses. From the early 1830s to the start of the Civil War, tariffs in the U.S. declined rather dramatically, until being raised, once more, to help fund the Civil War. (See chart on the next page.)

The combination of tariffs being sources of revenue and protectionist measures persisted after the Civil War. Did those tariffs play a role in supporting U.S. industrialization and growth, as claimed by their supporters? It's hard to make the case that certain U.S. businesses and industries innovated and grew due to being shielded from competition. Indeed, government action to limit competition would push in the exact opposite direction.

Irwin reported:

> Were high import tariffs somehow related to the strong U.S. economic growth during the late nineteenth century? One paper investigates the multiple channels by which tariffs could have promoted growth during this period. I found that 1) late nineteenth century growth hinged more on population expansion and capital accumulation than on productivity growth; 2)

tariffs may have discouraged capital accumulation by raising the price of imported capital goods; and 3) productivity growth was most rapid in non-traded sectors (such as utilities and services) whose performance was not directly related to the tariff.

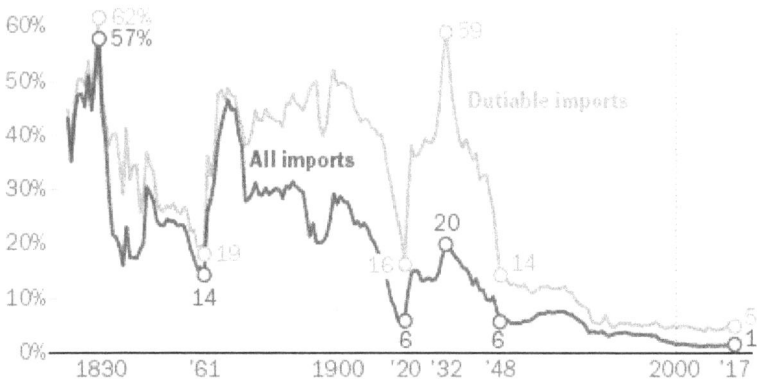

Source: Pew Research Center, "U.S. tariffs are among the lowest in the world – and in the nation's history," March 2018.

Finally, it's important to keep in mind the consequences when protectionism last held sway after World War I. Congress passed large tariff increases in the Emergency Tariff Act in 1921 and the Fordney-McCumber Tariff in 1922. U.S. exports actually declined by 46 percent from 1920 to 1921, and then declined by another 10 percent in 1922.

Free Trade Rocks! 45

Meanwhile, U.S. imports dropped by 50 percent from 1920 to 1921. Neither exports nor imports returned to their 1920 levels until World War II (in 1942 and 1943, respectively), and that's in nominal dollars (not adjusted for inflation). However, it also must be noted that trade resumed growth in 1923 and through 1929. It was in 1930 that Congress passed and President Herbert Hoover signed into law – against the advice of more than 1,000 economists – the Smoot-Hawley Tariff Act. (Again, see the chart on the previous page.) That notorious legislation jacked up tariffs and helped push the U.S. and the globe into the Great Depression, as trade collapsed in a trade war.

In fact, contrary to assertions by many historians, the Great Depression was not a failure of the free market. The trigger point was protectionism. The stock market grew jittery as Congress debated a massive increase in tariffs. As it looked more likely that the now-infamous Smoot-Hawley Tariff Act would become law, the stock market crashed in October 1929.

Hoover signed the Smoot-Hawley bill in June 1930. Again, after being set back by higher tariffs in the early 1920s, U.S. exports had resumed growing – from less than $5 billion in 1922 to more than $7 billion in 1929. Imports went from $3.4 billion in 1921 to almost $6 billion in 1929. But the Hoover-Smoot-Hawley tariff increases unleashed a trade war.

As the U.S. International Trade Commission noted ("U.S. Trade Policy since 1934"):

> International retaliatory moves led to a dramatic decline in the volume of world trade. Such actions included an increase in tariffs by the United Kingdom, prohibitive Italian tariffs on automobiles, significantly increased Spanish duties on products largely imported from the United States (e.g., automobiles, tires, tubes, and motion pictures), and similar Canadian actions against U.S. imports.

Indeed, global trade collapsed. By 1933, U.S. exports had plummeted by 66 percent compared to 1929 levels, and imports crashed by 70 percent from 1929 to 1933.

These protectionist ills were made far worse by both Presidents Hoover and Franklin D. Roosevelt's major increases in taxes and regulations, as well as unprecedented jumps in federal government spending.

Particularly after World War II, however, the U.S. largely took the global lead on reducing barriers to trade. We'll take a quick look at U.S. free trade agreements in a moment. For now, it's simply worth pointing out that U.S. longtime leadership in advancing free trade has been (at the time of this writing in 2019) abandoned during the presidency of Donald Trump in favor of a protectionist agenda.

As noted earlier, Barack Obama campaigned in 2008 on a protectionist message, but largely moved to the sidelines on trade after taking office. Donald Trump aggressively campaigned against free trade agreements, and governed that way.

In fact, the Trump administration veered into dangerous trade policy territory on Day One when the president withdrew the U.S. from negotiating the Trans-Pacific Partnership trade accord with 11 Asia-Pacific countries (Australia, Brunei, Canada, Chile, Japan, Malaysia, Mexico, New Zealand, Peru, Singapore, and Vietnam). The TPP would have eliminated tariffs on 18,000 U.S. exported goods and services. Subsequently, trade policy was focused on increasing tariffs on an assortment of goods, especially from China, as well as flirtations with killing the North American Free Trade Agreement (with a revised NAFTA, or US-Mexico-Canada Agreement (USMCA), awaiting votes by lawmakers in the U.S., Mexico and Canada at the time of this writing).

While imposing tariffs on Chinese imports, President Trump often claimed that China was paying those tariffs. In reality, though, U.S. consumers and businesses ultimately foot the bill for higher tariffs. Consumers face higher prices thanks to the tariffs and the corresponding ability for U.S. companies to raise prices. Choices are reduced as well.

Also, it often is noted that since between 53 percent and 61 percent of U.S. imports are inputs for U.S. businesses – that is, intermediary or capital goods – costs for U.S. firms rise, such as for manufacturing businesses. However, economist Don Boudreaux makes the point that practically all imports are inputs to U.S. businesses. In an August 2016 analysis ("All Imports Are Inputs") at CafeHayek.com, Boudreaux explained:

> The point is that nearly *all* imports that are not raw materials are appropriately classified as intermediate components. Thus, the percentage of American imports that together comprise the category "intermediate components or raw materials" is far larger than 50 percent. Indeed, it's likely well over 95 percent. Except for vacation travel abroad and the consumer goods and services that American vacationers purchase abroad, nearly all American imports – even of goods formally classified as consumer goods – are *inputs* into the production of producers in America.
>
> Consider, for example, a truckload of individually packaged bed linen imported into America from China. And to make matters simpler (although this assumption is unnecessary), assume – likely contrary to fact – that no American-supplied cotton or other inputs, at any stage of production, went into making these packages of bed linen. Suppose, reasonably, that these packages of bed linen will be offered for sale to final consumers in Wal-Mart stores throughout the United States.

These packages of bed linen are classified as consumer goods. They are, therefore, not among the greater-than-50-percent of American imports that are conventionally classified as intermediate components or raw materials. Yet I submit that this conventional classification is mistaken. These packages of bed linen, when unloaded on an American dock, are not sold directly to final consumers. They are sold to (or have already been purchased by) Wal-Mart. *These packages of bed linen are intermediate goods; they are inputs into Wal-Mart's production process.*

Wal-Mart produces retail services. Among the inputs that a producer of retail services must purchase are inventories to be used to stock its stores' shelves. So when Wal-Mart imports packaged bed linen, it does not buy these goods as consumer goods; it buys them as intermediate goods – goods that are used by Wal-Mart as inputs into producing the final consumer service that we might call "shopping convenience." Only by supplying this latter service – shopping convenience – does Wal-Mart earn profits. From Wal-Mart's perspective, imports from China of packaged bed linen are inputs used to produce its own output no less so than are Wal-Mart's delivery trucks, warehouses, cash registers, advertising, and corporate stationery.

In addition, part of the cost of tariffs is paid in the form of retaliatory measures taken by other nations against U.S. exports, which means lost business for those firms and their workers.

What becomes clear from the data and various studies are that the costs of protectionism often are substantial, while the presumed benefits espoused by protectionists – such as protection spurring certain industries forward – fail to hold up to serious analysis.

Make no mistake, U.S. consumers, workers and businesses pay for U.S. tariffs. That's just the straightforward economics. Indeed, while free trade rocks, protectionism sucks!

Point 8:
Brief History
of Free Trade Deals

Not long after the Smoot-Hawley Tariff Act of 1930, the U.S. began turning away from protectionism through an assortment of trade laws and deals. This period of reducing trade barriers and expanding free trade certainly was not a straight line – with many protectionist diversions or setbacks along the way – but it did largely hold sway for some 80-plus years.

The first step away from protectionism was the Reciprocal Trade Agreements Act of 1934 (RTAA), which set up the bargaining tariff whereby U.S. tariff relief was extended to nations that provided such relief to U.S. exporters.

After World War II, the Reciprocal Trade Act was extended. Economist Victor Canto, writing in the Winter 1983/84 *Cato Journal* ("U.S. Trade Policy: History and Evidence") noted that while there were problems with the Trade Agreements Act, with its extensions, "the United States signed bilateral trade agreements with 20 foreign nations." However, as noted by the U.S. International Trade Commission ("U.S. Trade Policy since 1934"), "The RTAA led to a series of bilateral tariff-reduction agreements, although these were not across-the-board cuts but rather selective reductions taking into account the possibility of injury to particular industries." Canto pointed out that "by 1947, tariff rates had been reduced to one-half their 1934 levels."

Free Trade Rocks! 51

President Truman signed the General Agreement on Tariffs and Trade (GATT) in 1947. GATT, largely under U.S. leadership, set up a multilateral process for negotiating tariff reductions. As noted in the chart in a previous chapter ("U.S. Average Tariff Rates (1821 to 2016)"), U.S. tariffs declined precipitously with various rounds of GATT talks held over the decades.

One major step forward for the U.S. was the Trade Expansion Act of 1962, led by President John F. Kennedy and passed by Congress, which authorized U.S. officials to negotiate tariff reductions up to 50 percent. The Kennedy Round (from 1962 to 1967) expanded free trade to more countries, with tariff reductions averaging 35 percent, according to the U.S. International Trade Commission. In fact, under GATT, relief from governmental-imposed barriers to trade proceeded under both Republican and Democratic presidents – after Kennedy, Presidents Lyndon B. Johnson, Richard Nixon, Gerald Ford, Jimmy Carter, Ronald Reagan, George H.W. Bush and Bill Clinton. The Uruguay Round, launched under Reagan and further advanced under Bush and Clinton, set up the World Trade Organization (WTO), and extended free trade rules to intellectual property protections, trade in services, and improved dispute resolutions.

As for the U.S. being engaged in bilateral and regional trade agreements, a significant step was taken under the Trade Act of 1974, whereby the president was granted "fast-track authority." Under fast-track (later renamed "trade promotion authority"), the president would negotiate a trade agreement, and Congress would take an up-or-down vote on the accord without any amendments. This provided trading partners assurance that any deal hammered out would not be altered due to special-interest pressures.

President Ronald Reagan got the U.S. rolling with the first bilateral free trade agreement going into effect with Israel in 1985, followed by an accord with Canada signed in 1988. Reagan called for other agreements, including a North

American accord and a free trade area covering the Western Hemisphere.

The North American effort was taken up by President George H.W. Bush. The North American Free Trade Agreement (NAFTA) was signed by Bush in December 1992; subsequently passed Congress and was signed into law in 1993 by President Clinton; and took effect in 1994.

While much maligned, like most other trade agreements, NAFTA was overwhelmingly about our trading partners reducing or eliminating their considerably higher trade barriers, given that the U.S. generally had much lower barriers. For example, Mexico's tariff levels prior to NAFTA were approximately three times larger on average than the United States'.

Since the free trade agreements went into effect with Canada, Mexico and the U.S., export growth from the U.S. to both nations has been strong. Again, the U.S. entered into a free trade agreement with Canada first, taking effect in 1989. From 1988 to 2018, U.S. goods exports to our neighbor to the north increased by 319 percent. (Over the same period, inflation – as measured by the GDP price index – increased by 87 percent.)

Export growth has been particularly strong with Mexico since NAFTA took effect in 1994. U.S. goods exports to Mexico grew by 538 percent from 1993 to 2018. (Inflation increased by only 60 percent over this period.)

Import growth was robust as well. Goods imports from Canada grew by 292 percent from 1988 to 2018, and goods imports from Mexico expanded by 767 percent from 1993 to 2018. Again, those imports include consumption goods as well as intermediate and capital goods, with U.S. consumers and businesses benefiting from the expanded choices and lower costs that come with lower barriers to imports.

Fast-track authority was allowed to lapse in 1993, and was not renewed until 2002 as "trade promotion authority." During that lapsed period, only one trade agreement was signed into law – the U.S.-Jordan Free Trade Agreement in 2001.

In December 2007, after both the U.S. House of Representatives and the Senate voted in favor, President George W. Bush signed the U.S.-Peru Trade Promotion Agreement into law. That marked the ninth free trade deal – covering a total of 14 nations – signed into law during the Bush administration. In addition, three deals signed by Bush eventually were tweaked and signed into law during the Obama administration – agreements with Colombia, South Korea and Panama. Clearly, the George W. Bush administration marked the greatest activity on free trade agreements under any U.S. president.

In mid-2007, however, trade promotion authority, once again, was not renewed. In addition, while vying for the Democratic Party's presidential nomination in 2008, Barack Obama declared his opposition to the pending trade deals with Colombia, South Korea and Panama, and declared a desire to renegotiate the 15-year-old North American Free Trade Agreement. It was a disturbing display of protectionist pandering for votes.

Once in the Oval Office, President Obama showed little interest in trade. Indeed, U.S. policymakers largely moved to the sidelines of global trade. Again, he eventually got around to sending the Colombia, South Korea and Panama accords to Congress for approval in 2011.

It was toward the end of President Obama's eight years in office when his administration finally became more proactive on trade by negotiating the Trans-Pacific Partnership trade accord. In February 2016, Obama signed the TPP, which, as noted earlier, would have eliminated some 18,000 tariffs imposed on U.S. goods and services. Still, Obama failed to put any real effort into getting the deal across the finish line in Congress.

That, of course, brings us to Donald Trump, who, again, pulled the U.S. out of the pending TPP as his first major act as president, and under his threat of walking away, renegotiated a NAFTA deal (which, again, had not yet been voted on by Congress at the time of this writing).

By the way, the TPP – renamed Comprehensive and Progressive Agreement for Trans-Pacific Partnership (CPTPP) – went into effect at the start of 2019 for seven of the 10 countries that had ratified the agreement at that point. The Canadian government has pointed out: "Once fully implemented, the 11 countries will form a trading bloc representing 495 million consumers and 13.5% of global GDP, providing Canada with preferential access to key markets in Asia and Latin America." Unfortunately, U.S. consumers, businesses and workers are left on the outside looking in, and working at a disadvantage in those markets.

Once again, economics and history make clear that protectionism sucks, and free trade rocks!

Point 9: The Morality of Free Trade

Throughout much of the history of mankind, life for most people was a daily struggle for survival. That changed markedly as the institutional foundations of the market economy were established and spread – with that process continuing today. Those institutions include establishing and protecting private property rights; competition; the rule of law; setting up tax and regulatory policies that incentivize entrepreneurship, investment and innovation; consumer sovereignty; and the freedom to trade. That freedom to trade, once again, pertains to transactions in the same town or village, throughout nations, and across international borders.

So, let's review key points making clear the moral superiority of free trade over protectionism.

First, there is an unmistakable moral component to establishing and expanding an economic system – that is, the market economy – essential to lifting people out of poverty; to the wealth creation that enables, for example, improved food production, housing, health care and overall quality of life; to greater leisure time; to a cleaner environment; and to incentivizing the private investment, innovation and exchange that allow for greater specialization, productivity and income growth. Free trade is central to the entire market process, and the free market is essential to economic and income growth, including poverty relief.

Second, the freedom to trade and exchange as one sees fit is a basic economic freedom that makes clear the value of each individual, with that same freedom serving to spur economic growth forward. Decades ago, my eighth grade teacher noted that the United States was the most prosperous country on the planet, yet she had no idea why that was the case. She failed to understand that it fundamentally was about economic freedom, that is, individuals being free to spend, save and invest their earnings as they see fit; free to start up, build and invest in businesses; free to gain education and skills needed to achieve their goals; and free to improve their lives by trading with whomever they choose.

Third, free trade points to individuals being able to improve their lives thanks to greater choices and lower prices in terms of consumption; thanks to enhanced productivity; thanks to a diffusion of technological advancements; and thanks to expanded opportunities by serving customers not only in their own town, state or country, but around the world. In contrast, protectionism is about the politically powerful influencing government in order to gain special treatment, such as U.S. steelmakers looking to be protected via tariffs or quotas. Such cronyism means that voluntary trade is being replaced by political dictates. It means that political power is reducing individual opportunity. When a country moves away from free trade, the people with lobbyists and political connections make out better than – and at the cost of – the average person.

Again, the Peterson Institute for International Economics found that benefits from expanded trade to the United States from 1950 to 2016 amounted to $2.1 trillion (measured in 2016 dollars), with per capita GDP and GDP per household growing by $7,014 and $18,131, respectively, with gains accruing disproportionately "to poorer households."

In terms of a global perspective, the World Bank and the World Trade Organization jointly published a report titled

Free Trade Rocks!

"The Role of Trade in Ending Poverty." A key message in that study was:

> People measure the value of trade by the extent to which it delivers better livelihoods, through higher incomes, greater choice, and a more sustainable future, among other benefits. For the extreme poor living on less than $1.25 a day, the central value of trade is its potential to help transform their lives and those of their families. In this way, there is no doubt that the integration of global markets through trade openness has made a critical contribution to poverty reduction. The number of people living in extreme poverty around the world has fallen by around one billion since 1990. Without the growing participation of developing countries in international trade, and sustained efforts to lower barriers to the integration of markets, it is hard to see how this reduction could have been achieved...
>
> Trade also affects long-term growth since it gives access to more advanced technological inputs available in the global market and because it enhances the incentives to innovate. Trade contributes directly to poverty reduction by opening up new employment opportunities, for example for agricultural producers, with the expansion of export sectors, and by bringing about structural changes in the economy that increase employment of low-skilled, poor workers in the informal sector. Trade also provides better access to external markets for the goods that the poor produce.

Finally, trade is not war – despite the rhetoric sometimes used by politicians who oppose free trade. Nor is free trade particularly about winners vs. losers – again, a politically favorite accusation hurled at times. In contrast, voluntary exchanges in a free market rank as the exact opposite of war, in any sense of the word. Each party gains in a market trade; if not, the exchange wouldn't occur.

For good measure, free trade works against actual war. After all, if individuals and businesses freely partake in commerce with individuals and businesses in another country, those two nations are less likely to go to war. Indeed, this was one of the reasons why there was such a push to reduce trade barriers after World War II – especially given that many saw restrictions on trade (that is, protectionism) during the 1920s and 1930s as a contributor to the outbreak of World War II.

Free trade does not mean that no one will lose a job or no business will fail. Quite the contrary, market competition means that consumers ultimately decide which products succeed and fail, and in turn, which businesses will succeed and fail. That, in turn, means that resources are allocated to their best or most efficient uses given the needs and demands of consumers. Competition remains essential to long-run economic growth. This stands in opposition to protectionism whereby politicians climb into bed with special interests to dole out dollars, and try to anoint winners and losers.

Free trade is about economic growth, lifting people out of poverty, creating wealth, boosting incomes, enhancing freedom, and mutually beneficial commerce. Free trade is a moral good, and yes, it rocks!

Point 10: The Future of Trade

When the economies of other countries grow, and their citizens' incomes rise, that's good news for everyone else around the world, including, most certainly, consumers, workers and businesses in the United States. As long as more countries embrace free markets, and establish the foundations upon which markets are built, a process of increased entrepreneurship, private investment, innovation, technological advancement, specialization, productivity, and trade will continue to drive prosperity forward into the future.

For example, it was reported in the May 2017 study from the Peterson Institute for International Economics:

> Estimated future gains that the United States might realize from fresh policy liberalization are $540 billion, implying that US GDP per capita could increase by $1,670, and US GDP per household could rise by $4,400 by 2025. These are potential gains from worldwide lower tariffs and reduced logistics costs on traded goods, and lower barriers to services trade. Substantial additional gains might be delivered by technological advances that reduce the cost of distance between countries.

Unfortunately, though, politicians have a knack for ignoring or being ignorant of sound economics. When pandering politics, for example, wins out over sound economics, markets and economic growth are undermined.

At the time of this writing, misguided politics dominated on the trade front with President Donald Trump. U.S. global leadership on advancing free trade, as we have seen, prevailed after World War II until it was diminished under President Obama and lost under the Trump administration.

Thankfully, though, no reason exists why the U.S. cannot reclaim its vital global leadership role in advancing free trade. That means leading by example. It means being a positive influence for the expansion of market economics and free trade.

For example, I testified before Congress in April 2018, and laid out a productive alternative to how the U.S. should deal with China on the trade front. Specifically, I testified:

> Meanwhile, the answer to dealing with China and its violations of intellectual property (IP), along with other governmental abuses, is not to impose tariffs and quotas that will only hurt U.S. consumers and small businesses.
>
> From a certain perspective, given that China technically remains a communist country, it has made notable advances in opening markets – as illustrated by the tremendous growth in U.S. exports to China and small businesses involved in China trade – but much more, to say the least, is needed.
>
> In the midst of this debate, it is important to understand that China is no longer the world's low-cost manufacturer, and the country is looking to shift to more value-added endeavors. However, that will not be accomplished by government dictates, protectionism, and/or intellectual property theft. Instead, it will require further economic freedom and stronger IP protections. Rather than playing tit-for-tat

protectionism, the U.S. would be far better off in standing up clearly for free markets, free trade and property rights, and showing other countries, like China, what the real path to economic growth is. It is critical, and far more constructive, to make clear to China that its intellectual property violations only serve to undermine its own investment and economic growth.

Rather than raising costs to trade with China, the best path forward would be to enter into serious discussions that lay the groundwork for a China-U.S. free trade agreement. Through that process, the U.S. would be able to constructively advance the cause for open markets and property rights in China. And a free trade accord between the world's two largest economies would considerably expand opportunities for entrepreneurs, small businesses and workers in both nations.

Advancing freedom – whether in the political sphere, the economic sphere, or both – is not easy. But it obviously is worth the mighty efforts.

Americans need to reject the fear, doubts and isolationism promoted by the ugly politics of both the Left's Progressivism and a populism growing on the Right. These movements often find their voices in protectionism.

This nation was built on a tax revolt – i.e., against taxation without representation – and that very much was about taxes, and other restrictions, on trade. In *American Heritage* (July-August 1993), historian John Steele Gordon noted:

> Interstate tariffs on American exports were specifically banned by the Constitution.

As a result, the United States began its independent existence with the freest internal market in the world, and it has largely maintained that freedom, at least relative to other countries. Having the greatest freedom to create wealth, American citizens have proceeded to do exactly that in vast abundance...

After the expensive British victory in the Seven Years' War (called the French and Indian War on this continent), the British government woke up to the fact that there was an economic giant aborning across the Atlantic. It tried to make it a source of serious revenue, mainly by taxing its trade. The result was the American Revolution.

Voters and politicians need to understand that whatever economic challenges the U.S. has confronted in recent years – specifically, during and after the Great Recession – these have not come about due to free trade, nor are they about technological advancements. Instead, the woes of recent times – in particular, under-performing economic growth compared to the historical average – find their roots in rather traditional places, namely, government policy gone awry, such as costly tax and regulatory burdens, large government draining resources from the private sector, and yes, misguided trade policies.

The U.S. must get back to sound economics on trade. That means, for example, moving forward with free trade agreements with China, the European Union, the United Kingdom, and Reagan's call for a Western Hemisphere free trade area, as well as the U.S. joining the Comprehensive and Progressive Agreement for Trans-Pacific Partnership. The United States must reclaim its leadership role, and once again, proclaim to and show the world that free trade rocks!

Bibliography

• American Farm Bureau, "Facts About Agriculture & Food," www.fb.org, accessed August 2019.

• Donald J. Boudreaux, "All Imports are Inputs," CafeHayek.com, August 4, 2016.

• Donald J. Boudreaux and Nita Ghei, "The Benefits of Free Trade: Addressing Key Myths," Mercatus Center, George Mason University, January 2017.

• Business Roundtable, *How the U.S. Economy Benefits from International Trade and Investment*, 2015.

• Victor Canto, "U.S. Trade Policy: History and Evidence," *Cato Journal*, Winter 1983/84.

• John Steele Gordon, "Land of Free Trade," *American Heritage*, Volume 44, Issue 4, 1993.

• Colin Grabow, "Candy-Coated Cartel: Time to Kill the U.S. Sugar Program," Cato Institute, *Policy Analysis No. 837*, April 10, 2018.

• Gary Clyde Hufbauer and Zhiyao (Lucy) Lu, "The Payoff to America from Globalization: A Fresh Look with a Focus on Costs to Workers," Peterson Institute for International Economics, May 2017.

• Douglas A. Irwin, "Historical Aspects of U.S. Trade Policy," National Bureau of Economic Research, Summer 2006.

• Arnold Kling, "International Trade," *The Concise Encyclopedia of Economics*, Econlib.org.

• N. Gregory Mankiw, "Beyond the Noise on Free Trade," *The New York Times*, March 16, 2008.

• Iain Murray and Ryan Young, *Traders of the Lost Ark: Rediscovering a Moral and Economic Case for Free Trade*, Competitive Enterprise Institute, August 2018.

• William Poole, "Free Trade: Why Are Economists and Noneconomists So Far Apart?" Federal Reserve Bank of St. Louis *Review*, September/October 2004.

• Richard W. Rahn, "Destructive Information," *The Washington Times*, March 26, 2018.

• Brian Reinbold and Yi Wen, "Historical U.S. Trade Deficits," Federal Reserve Bank of St. Louis, May 2019.

• David Riker, *Export-Intensive Industries Pay More on Average: An Update*, U.S. International Trade Commission, April 2015.

• Adam Smith, *An Inquiry into the Nature and Causes of the Wealth of Nations*, 1776.

• U.S. Chamber of Commerce, Consumer Electronics Association, National Retail Federation, and American Apparel and Footwear Association, *Imports Work for America*, May 2013.

• U.S. International Trade Commission, "U.S. Trade Policy since 1934," 2009.

• Daniel Workman, "United States Top 10 Exports," WorldTopExports.com, August 21, 2019.

• World Bank Group and World Trade Organization, *The Role of Trade in Ending Poverty*, 2015.

Suggested Further Reading

For those interested in reading more about international trade, there are many wonderful books, studies and articles. Here are but a few for your consideration:

- Henry Hazlitt, *Economics in One Lesson*, 1946.

- Douglas A. Irwin, *Against the Tide: An Intellectual History of Free Trade*, Princeton University Press, 1997.

- Pierre Lemieux, *What's Wrong with Protectionism*, Mercatus Center, George Mason University, August 2018.

- Russell Roberts, *The Choice: A Fable of Free Trade and Protection*, Pearson, 2006.

- Adam Smith, *An Inquiry into the Nature and Causes of the Wealth of Nations*, 1776.

About the Author

Ray Keating is an economist, columnist, podcaster, editor, publisher, entrepreneur, and author of a variety of nonfiction and fiction books.

He serves as chief economist for the Small Business & Entrepreneurship Council (the views expressed in this and his other books, by the way, are his own).

In addition, Keating is the editor/publisher/columnist for DisneyBizJournal.com. Keating was a columnist with RealClearMarkets.com, and a former weekly columnist for *Newsday*, *Long Island Business News*, and the *New York City Tribune*. His work has appeared in a wide range of additional periodicals, including *The New York Times*, *The Wall Street Journal*, *The Washington Post*, *New York Post*, *Los Angeles Daily News*, *The Boston Globe*, *National Review*, *The Washington Times*, *Investor's Business Daily*, *New York Daily News*, *Detroit Free Press*, *Chicago Tribune*, *Providence Journal Bulletin*, *TheHill.com*, *Touchstone* magazine, *Townhall.com*, *Newsmax*, and *Cincinnati Enquirer*.

Keating also has written 11 thrillers/mysteries in his Pastor Stephen Grant series. The first eight novels are *Warrior Monk*, followed by *Root of All Evil?*, *An Advent for Religious Liberty*, *The River*, *Murderer's Row*, *Wine Into Water*,

Lionhearts, and *Reagan Country*, followed by the short stories *Heroes and Villains* and *Shifting Sands*, and then another novel, *Deep Rough*. A second edition of *Warrior Monk*, with a new Author Introduction and a new Epilogue, was published in early 2019 as well.

Enjoy All of the Pastor Stephen Grant Adventures!

Paperbacks and Kindle versions at Amazon.com

Signed books at raykeatingonline.com

• ***Deep Rough: A Pastor Stephen Grant Novel*** **by Ray Keating**

One man faces challenges as a pastor in China. His son has become a breakout phenom in the world of professional golf. The Chinese government is displeased with both, and their lives are in danger. Stephen Grant – onetime Navy SEAL, former CIA operative and current pastor – has a history with the communist Chinese, while also claiming a pretty solid golf game. His unique experience and skills unexpectedly put him alongside old friends; at some of golf's biggest tournaments as a caddy and bodyguard; and in the middle of an international struggle over Christian persecution, a mission of revenge, and a battle between good and evil.

• ***Shifting Sands: A Pastor Stephen Grant Short Story*** **by Ray Keating**

Beach volleyball is about fun, sun and sand. But when a big-time tournament arrives on a pier in New York City, danger and international intrigue are added to the mix. Stephen Grant, a former Navy SEAL, onetime CIA operative, and current pastor, is on the scene with his wife, friends and former CIA colleagues. While battles on the volleyball court play out, deadly struggles between good and evil are engaged on and off the sand.

• ***Heroes and Villains: A Pastor Stephen Grant Short Story*** **by Ray Keating**

As a onetime Navy SEAL, a former CIA operative and a pastor, many people call Stephen Grant a hero. At various times defending the Christian Church and the United States over the years, he has journeyed across the nation and around the world. But now Grant finds himself in an entirely unfamiliar setting – a comic book, science fiction and fantasy convention. But he still joins forces with a unique set of heroes in an attempt to foil a villainous plot against one of the all-time great comic book writers and artists.

• ***Reagan Country: A Pastor Stephen Grant Novel*** **by Ray Keating**

Could President Ronald Reagan's influence reach into the former "evil empire"? The media refers to a businessman on the rise as "Russia's Reagan." Unfortunately, others seek a return to the old ways, longing for Russia's former "greatness." The dispute becomes deadly. Conflict stretches from the Reagan Presidential Library in California to the White House to a Russian Orthodox monastery to the

Kremlin. Stephen Grant, pastor at St. Mary's Lutheran Church on Long Island, a former Navy SEAL and onetime CIA operative, stands at the center of the tumult.

- *Lionhearts: A Pastor Stephen Grant Novel* by Ray Keating

War has arrived on American soil, with Islamic terrorists using new tactics. Few are safe, including Christians, politicians, and the media. Pastor Stephen Grant taps into his past with the Navy SEALS and the CIA to help wage a war of flesh and blood, ideas, history, and beliefs. This is about defending both the U.S. and Christianity.

- *Wine Into Water: A Pastor Stephen Grant Novel* by Ray Keating

Blood, wine, sin, justice and forgiveness... Who knew the wine business could be so sordid and violent? That's what happens when it's infiltrated by counterfeiters. A pastor, once a Navy SEAL and CIA operative, is pulled into action to help unravel a mystery involving fake wine, murder and revenge. Stephen Grant is called to take on evil, while staying rooted in his life as a pastor.

- *Murderer's Row: A Pastor Stephen Grant Novel* by Ray Keating

How do rescuing a Christian family from the clutches of Islamic terrorists, minor league baseball in New York, a string of grisly murders, sordid politics, and a pastor, who once was a Navy SEAL and CIA operative, tie together? *Murderer's Row* is the fifth Pastor Stephen Grant novel, and Keating serves up fascinating characters, gripping adventure, and a tangled murder mystery, along with faith, politics, humor, and, yes, baseball.

- ***The River: A Pastor Stephen Grant Novel*** **by Ray Keating**

Some refer to Las Vegas as Sin City. But the sins being committed in *The River* are not what one might typically expect. Rather, it's about murder. Stephen Grant once used lethal skills for the Navy SEALs and the CIA. Now, years later, he's a pastor. How does this man of action and faith react when his wife is kidnapped, a deep mystery must be untangled, and both allies and suspects from his CIA days arrive on the scene? How far can Grant go – or will he go – to save the woman he loves? Will he seek justice or revenge, and can he tell the difference any longer?

- ***An Advent for Religious Liberty: A Pastor Stephen Grant Novel*** **by Ray Keating**

Advent and Christmas approach. It's supposed to be a special season for Christians. But it's different this time in New York City. Religious liberty is under assault. The Catholic Church has been called a "hate group." And it's the newly elected mayor of New York City who has set off this religious and political firestorm. Some people react with prayer – others with violence and murder. Stephen Grant, former CIA operative turned pastor, faces deadly challenges during what becomes known as "An Advent for Religious Liberty." Grant works with the cardinal who leads the Archdiocese of New York, the FBI, current friends, and former CIA colleagues to fight for religious liberty, and against dangers both spiritual and physical.

- *Root of All Evil? A Pastor Stephen Grant Novel* by **Ray Keating**

Do God, politics and money mix? In *Root of All Evil?*, the combination can turn out quite deadly. Keating introduced readers to Stephen Grant, a former CIA operative and current parish pastor, in the fun and highly praised *Warrior Monk*. Now, Grant is back in *Root of All Evil?* It's a breathtaking thriller involving drug traffickers, politicians, the CIA and FBI, a shadowy foreign regime, the Church, and money. Charity, envy and greed are on display. Throughout, action runs high.

- *Warrior Monk: A Pastor Stephen Grant Novel* by **Ray Keating**

Warrior Monk revolves around a former CIA assassin, Stephen Grant, who has lived a far different, relatively quiet life as a parish pastor in recent years. However, a shooting at his church, a historic papal proposal, and threats to the pope's life mean that Grant's former and current lives collide. Grant must tap the varied skills learned as a government agent, a theologian and a pastor not only to protect the pope, but also to feel his way through a minefield of personal challenges. The second edition of *Warrior Monk* includes a new Introduction by Ray Keating, as well as a new Epilogue that points to an upcoming Pastor Stephen Grant novel.

All of the Pastor Stephen Grant novels are available at Amazon.com and signed books at www.raykeatingonline.com.

The Traitor is Coming!

Join the Pastor Stephen Grant Novels & Short Stories Email List, and Get
The Traitor:
A Pastor Stephen Grant Short Story
for FREE!

If you join the Pastor Stephen Grant Novels & Short Stories Email List, you'll receive Pastor Stephen Grant stuff, including a newsletter, and a FREE ebook copy of the forthcoming Pastor Stephen Grant short story titled THE TRAITOR.

Join now by quickly filling out the contact information at

http://www.pastorstephengrant.com/contact.html

Join the Pastor Stephen Grant Fellowship!

Visit
www.patreon.com/pastorstephengrantfellowship

Consider joining the Pastor Stephen Grant Fellowship to enjoy the Pastor Stephen Grant and the related novels, receive new short stories, earn special thanks, gain access to even more content, receive fun gifts, and perhaps even have a character named after you, a friend or a loved one.

Ray Keating declares, "I've always said that I'll keep writing as long as someone wants to read what I write. Thanks to reader support from this Patreon effort, I will be able to pen more Pastor Stephen Grant and related novels, while also generating short stories, reader guides, and other fun material. At various levels of support, you can become an essential part of making this happen, while getting to read everything that is written before the rest of the world, and earning other exclusive benefits – some that are pretty darn cool!"

Readers can join at various levels…

- **Reader Level at $4.99 per month…**

You receive all new novels FREE and earlier than the rest of the world, and you get FREE exclusive, early reads of new Pastor Stephen Grant short stories throughout the year. In addition, your name is included in a special "Thank You" section in forthcoming novels, and you gain access to the private Pastor Stephen Grant Fellowship Facebook page, which includes daily journal entries from Pastor Stephen Grant, insights from other characters, regular recipes from Grillin' with the Monks, periodic videos and Q&A's with Ray Keating, and more!

• **Bronze Reader Level at $9.99 per month…**

All the benefits from the above level, plus you receive two special gift boxes throughout the year with fun and exclusive Pastor Stephen Grant merchandise.

• **Silver Reader Level at $22.99 per month…**

All the benefits from the above levels, plus you receive two additional (for a total of four) special gift boxes throughout the year with fun and exclusive Pastor Stephen Grant merchandise, and you get a signed, personalized (signed to you or the person of your choice as a gift) Pastor Stephen Grant novel three times a year.

• **Gold Reader Level at $39.99 per month…**

All the benefits from the above levels, plus your name or the name of someone you choose to be used for a character in <u>one</u> upcoming novel.

• **Ultimate Reader Level at $49.99 per month…**

All the benefits from the above levels, plus your name or the name of someone you choose (in addition to the one named under the Gold level!) to be used for a <u>major recurring character</u> in upcoming novels.

Visit www.patreon.com/pastorstephengrantfellowship

Sign up for Ray Keating's "Free Enterprise, Entrepreneurship, Writing, Disney and More" Email List!

Enjoy Great Deals

Receive free newsletters and updates, notifications about events, and 40% off coupons for all of Keating's forthcoming books covering entrepreneurship, business, your career, writing, Disney, TO DO list solutions, and more!

Upcoming books scheduled for publication include:

- *10 Entrepreneurship Lessons from Walt Disney*
- *10 Entrepreneurship Lessons for Writers*
- *The Realistic Optimist Planner 2020: The TO DO List Solution*
- *The Disney Planner 2020: The TO DO List Solution*
- *The Movie Buff Planner 2020: The TO DO List Solution*
- *The Lutheran Planner 2020: The TO DO List Solution*

Sign up at https://raykeatingonline.com/contact

Visit DisneyBizJournal.com

News, Analysis and Reviews of the Disney Entertainment Business!

DisneyBizJournal.com is a media site providing news, information and analysis for anyone who has an interest in the Walt Disney Company, and its assorted ventures, operations, and history. Fans (Disney, Pixar, Marvel, Star Wars, Indiana Jones, and more), investors, entrepreneurs, executives, teachers, professors and students will find valuable information, analysis, and commentary in its pages.

DisneyBizJournal.com is run by Ray Keating, who has experience as a newspaper and online columnist, economist, business teacher and speaker, novelist, movie and book reviewer, podcaster, and more.

Free Enterprise in Three Minutes Podcast with Ray Keating

This podcast provides three-minute (give or take a few seconds) answers to important questions about free enterprise, the economy, business and related issues. Ray Keating cuts through the economic mumbo-jumbo, tosses aside the economic mistakes often made in the media and in political circles, and quickly gets at economic reality. Who says free enterprise and economics have to be mind-numbing? That's not the case with Free Enterprise in Three Minutes with Ray Keating.

Listen in and subscribe at iTunes, or on Buzzsprout at http://www.buzzsprout.com/155969.

Ray Keating's Authors and Entrepreneurs Podcast

This entertaining podcast is geared toward readers, aspiring authors, entrepreneurs, and aspiring entrepreneurs. It explores the world of authors as entrepreneurs. The podcast discusses the creative and business aspects of being a writer, and what that means for authors themselves as well as for the reading public. Keating serves up assorted insights and ideas.

Listen in and subscribe at iTunes, or on Buzzsprout at http://www.buzzsprout.com/147907.

Ray Keating's Services for Authors and Entrepreneurs

- **A Business Plan – An Action Plan – for Your Book**

Ray Keating will read your manuscript and provide a personalized, 12-point business plan for your book. That plan will cover such areas as

- identifying your market;
- ideas for using social media to promote your book and interact with readers;
- a personalized media release for your book created by Ray Keating;
- suggested advertising options based on various budgets;
- specific actions you can take for working with the media;
- identifying a variety of promotional tools that fit with your book;
- steps for identifying speaking opportunities;
- and more, depending on the specifics of your book.

This is a plan of action for your book – a roadmap for you to follow.

If you're an author, then you are an entrepreneur. That's the message Ray Keating communicates in his Authors and Entrepreneurs Podcast and to fellow writers, and it's the reality that he executes with each of his own books.

As an author and entrepreneur, you need a business plan – that is, an action plan – for your book. That's where Ray Keating is able to help fellow authors on an individualized basis.

While most authors enjoy writing their book, many are unsure about the business aspects of being an author. Specifically, they're uncertain about or uncomfortable with what's needed to get their books into the marketplace, that is, into the hands of readers. Ray Keating's personalized business plan for your book offer a roadmap to assist you, the author, in becoming a better entrepreneur when it comes to your book.

We know what authors do. They, of course, write.

But what's an entrepreneur? An entrepreneur both owns and operates a business. Entrepreneurs are not passive shareholders. They're not managers for someone else who is the owner. Entrepreneurs both own and actively run their businesses. That's also what authors do. Creating a book is very much like launching a startup business. Authors' creations are their products. And no matter whom authors work with, authors own their books. Their books, in effect, are their businesses.

Ray Keating notes, "My impression is that most writers don't like the business end of things. But if an author is serious about setting and reaching sales goals, no matter how big or small, then every author needs to embrace the role of the entrepreneur. Entrepreneurs own and operate their own businesses. That's exactly what authors do. Your books are your passion, your creations and your business. You are the owner and operator of your books, if you will, and you need to work for their success. You need a business plan for your book."

Whether you've written several books, or this is your first, every book needs a business plan.

Whether you are going the route of traditional or indie publishing, you need a business plan – an action plan – for your book.

Visit https://raykeatingonline.com/t/authorsandentrepreneurs for more information and pricing.

- **Manuscript Assessment and Feedback on Your Book**

Ray Keating will read your book, and provide an "Assessment and Feedback" memo that offers thorough thoughts and suggestions, such as on story, plot, characters, dialogue, clarity, consistency and structure. Throughout his career in writing, business and teaching, Keating has always appreciated constructive feedback for his own efforts, and believes that such feedback is critical for authors and entrepreneurs. Ray Keating's "Assessment and Feedback" service focuses on the complete book, pointing out the positives and suggested areas for improvement.

Visit https://raykeatingonline.com/t/authorsandentrepreneurs for more information and pricing.

- **Copyediting for Your Book**

Perhaps your book simply needs a quality round of copyediting. Ray Keating offers that service as well. The copyedit will not touch the content of your book, but instead will focus on issues like spelling, punctuation, grammar, terminology, and capitalization, along with matters of continuity when it comes to plot and characters. This is especially critical for authors who plan to take the indie or self-publishing path.

Visit https://raykeatingonline.com/t/authorsandentrepreneurs for more information and pricing.

Unleashing Small Business Through IP: The Role of Intellectual Property in Driving Entrepreneurship, Innovation and Investment

In today's global economy, the protection of intellectual property (IP) is especially critical for small businesses and entrepreneurs. No matter what industry or line of business - from local shops to manufacturers, internet ventures to songwriters, fashion designers to specialty food makers - IP matters to the growth and competitiveness of the entrepreneurial sector. In the second edition of *Unleashing Small Business Through IP*, Ray Keating provides insights and hard data on the role of IP in our economy. This book reveals the heavy costs associated with IP theft, and IP's impact on innovation, entrepreneurship, investment and quality job creation. In our increasingly competitive yet interdependent global economy, the establishment and enforcement of IP rights is essential for all of its players - and especially small business.

Get signed books at www.raykeatingonline.com, and paperbacks and the Kindle edition at Amazon.com.

"Chuck" vs. the Business World: Business Tips on TV by Ray Keating

Paperbacks and for the Kindle at Amazon.com

Signed books at raykeatingonline.com

Among Ray Keating's nonfiction books is *"Chuck" vs. the Business World: Business Tips on TV.*

In this book, Keating finds career advice, and lessons on managing or owning a business in a fun, fascinating and unexpected place, that is, in the television show *Chuck*.

Keating shows that TV spies and nerds can provide insights and guidelines on managing workers, customer relations, leadership, technology, hiring and firing people, and balancing work and personal life.

Larry Kudlow of CNBC says, "Ray Keating has taken the very funny television series *Chuck*, and derived some valuable lessons and insights for your career and business."

If you love *Chuck*, you'll love this book. And even if you never watched *Chuck*, the book lays out clear examples and quick lessons from which you can reap rewards.

Check out the following excerpt – Chapter 20 – from *Chuck*...

> *"I often think about meats and cheeses."*
>
> - Lou

20
Lou Versus Lester: The Passion of the Entrepreneur

    Entrepreneurship and the investment that fuels such crucial risk taking are what drive the economy forward.
    No matter how big a business gets – including such current-day leaders as Wal-Mart, Microsoft and Apple – each was at one time a small, entrepreneurial venture. For good measure, most businesses in the U.S. are smaller firms. The Small Business Administration's Office of Advocacy has reported, for example, that of the 27.5 million businesses in the U.S. in 2009, 99.9 percent had fewer than 500 workers.
    In *Chuck's* first four seasons, only one true entrepreneur was introduced, while another regular character had

entrepreneurial dreams, but lacked the common sense needed by entrepreneurs.

• A woman named Lou enters the Buy More with a cellphone that is not working. Lou is freaking out because, as she puts it, "my entire life is in this thing." (Season 1, Episode 8: "Chuck Versus the Truth")

Chuck tries to calm her, saying she can trust him to fix it. When Lou again starts to get upset, he advises, "No, no, don't go there. Come back. Go to a happy place. Is there something that you think about that quiets the voices that are in your head?"

Lou says, "Turkey, muenster cheese, egg bread, grilled."

Chuck asks, "Was that a sandwich?"

Lou responds, "Yeah, they're my passion."

"It sounds pretty delicious," says Chuck.

Lou declares, "I own a deli in the mall. I often think about meats and cheeses."

• When the Jeffster band is playing outside the Buy More, Big Mike observes, "That's quite a wad of cash you hustled on Buy More property."

Lester responds, "Whoa, this is our dream. We're on break. You can't touch us."

Big Mike says, "I don't want to touch you. I want to help you. In case you forgot, I know a thing or two about management. You're too good to be playing outside a chain electronic store. If I was your manager, you might be playing inside a chain electronic store."

Lester responds, "Yeah, we've already played the Buy More. We don't need you."

But Jeff says, "I'm listening… having a manager means having respect."

Lester warns, "How many times do I have to tell you? Art: good. Commercialism: bad, evil, weird, chubby."

Lester then walks away from Jeffster.

Free Trade Rocks! 89

Later, Big Mike tries to assure Lester: "I'm a man, a man who once had a dream, too. You ever heard of Earth, Wind & Fire?"

Lester nods, "Yeah, they jammed."

Big Mike tells him: "For a short time in 1988, we were called Earth, Wind, Fire & Rain. I was Rain."

Impressed, Lester finally says, "Where do I sign?"

Chuck Business Tips

When I'm in the midst of marketing and selling a book, my oldest son often jokes by shaking his head and declaring, "You're going commercial."

My response? "Darn right, I'm trying to go commercial."

The point of any entrepreneurial venture is to go commercial, if by "commercial" one means trying to appeal to and generate a large volume of sales from the largest number of consumers. After all, the point is success.

"Going commercial" also does not necessarily mean diminishing the artistic quality of one's product or service. After all, consumers ultimately want the best product for the best price.

Lester doesn't grasp this notion. He wants success, but is unwilling to take the steps needed to achieve it. Of course, the fundamental problem is that Jeffster isn't any good as a band.

Lou, however, is the type of entrepreneur who understands what it takes to go commercial. She is passionate about her deli, and obviously works to offer customers the best sandwiches around.

Indeed, Lou is willing to go above and beyond to get the best ingredients, as illustrated when she illegally imports salami, in order to get around government customs regulations that make no sense, to get the tastiest meats. Even as he goes off to save Chuck and Sarah, Casey takes a second to tell Lou: "By the way, miss. Your pastrami's delicious." (Season 1, Episode 8: "Chuck Versus the Imported Hard Salami")

Lou is a passionate and smart entrepreneur.

Get signed books at www.raykeatingonline.com, and paperbacks and the Kindle edition at Amazon.com.

www.ingramcontent.com/pod-product-compliance
Lightning Source LLC
Chambersburg PA
CBHW070427220526
45466CB00004B/1573